A GARDENER'S GUIDE TO

HEDGES
AND LIVING
BOUNDARIES

Selection, planting and maintenance

A GARDENER'S GUIDE TO
HEDGES
AND LIVING
BOUNDARIES

Selection, planting and maintenance

ROGER HIRONS

 THE CROWOOD PRESS

First published in 2022 by
The Crowood Press Ltd
Ramsbury, Marlborough
Wiltshire SN8 2HR

enquiries@crowood.com

www.crowood.com

British Library Cataloguing-in-Publication Data
A catalogue record for this book is available from the British Library.

ISBN 978 0 7198 4125 5

Typeset by Simon and Sons
Cover design by Blue Sunflower Creative
Printed and bound in India by Parksons Graphics

CONTENTS

INTRODUCTION

Welcome to the journey of selecting the correct boundary choice for your client and their neighbour, or for yourself and your neighbour. Whatever you decide to plant as a living divide will affect at least one person who lives on the other side of that planting. Of course, creating an internal divide within your own grounds will not have an impact on anyone else, but it will affect the surrounding plants and therefore wise choices are still required. When the right plants and structure are chosen, the result will be a joy to look at as well as to look after – and the neighbour will agree. When the incorrect choice has been implemented, this is when neighbours can fall out.

With this in mind, it is sensible to begin any project by talking to your neighbour or your client's neighbour about the sort of planting you are looking to use. As with everything, a little communication can go a long way. The other major consideration when selecting plants is the amount of time that will be available for maintenance. Time inevitably moves on alarmingly quickly when you have a busy life and a living divide that requires lots of tying in or pruning regularly can soon be abandoned. Some plants can recover from irregular care, but others will never be the same again if neglect has gone too far.

The aim of this book is to impart some of my knowledge, gained through 35 years' experience in the industry, to reduce the number of mistakes that can happen when creating a living divide. Choosing the wrong plants can prove to be costly in the long run, both in terms of money and time, and few people can afford to be wasteful in this way. However, as far as is possible, concerns over expenditure should not be allowed to get in the way of purchasing the right plant, which may well outlive both garden designer and owner. Many mature gardens have been planted over time, sometimes over several generations. With careful consideration, you should be able to make an informed choice and achieve a good result that will stand the test of time.

Another important consideration is the provision of a habitat for wildlife. This is a subject close to my heart – I believe we have a duty to look after what we have been given. Back in the 1990s it was suggested that everyone with a garden should devote a quarter of it to measures to encourage wildlife. Ever-increasing infrastructure, especially in urban areas, has led to the destruction of habitats. Water displacement, caused by hard surfaces being cambered towards main drain systems, has had a direct negative influence on the diversity of flora and fauna, as water that should be allocated to green areas is directed away to somewhere else. A living divide can create a wonderful natural corridor that can harbour a huge and diverse range of insects, birds and small mammals. Looking after the base of the food chain will directly contribute to the survival of wildlife in urban spaces.

A few years ago, I was commissioned to landscape part of the rear garden to a fairly new house. It incorporated a mixed hedge that was more than fifty years old, with big rocks along its base. As I trudged back and forth with tons of mulch and soil in my wheelbarrow, a tiny dormouse came and sat on one of these rocks and watched me. Apparently, when the new houses in that area had been built, the local authority had insisted that the old hedgerow be kept. Their approach is to be applauded, allowing wildlife to be preserved within urban spaces.

When you first plant a new living divide, it will take time for the wildlife to move in. However, as it matures, it will start to create a decent habitat. All living creatures need to be able to feed and to find shelter. In the ideal scenario, there would be small holes, roughly six inches square, at the base of a few random fences or solid boundaries in everyone's garden, and a living boundary in front of these inert divides. This would create a labyrinth of corridors, connecting to one another, which could be used by birds and hedgehogs and other small mammals. The base of the living divide will change each year, with the seasons, and if that part of the system is left alone, then the insects and creepy crawlies will have a home, giving the small birds and small mammals something to live off.

A mixed hedge can be planted either primarily for humans to enjoy, or specifically to increase the diversity of insect and creature within the garden – or as a combination of both. The first version will produce fruit that can be made into edible products. If you go down this route, do some research into recipes in advance of planting, to determine which ingredients will be the most useful, and then plant more of them to maximize pollination and therefore get more fruit. Prioritizing the support of wildlife is the responsible option. It will be extremely rewarding, and is especially important in urban areas, where living things have been increasingly replaced with inert features. It is possible to compensate somewhat for the imbalance by planting up walls and fences with the correct plants, but the best way is to create an entire living boundary. My hope is that this book will help you to do this, and that the result will be the survival and preservation of lots of wild creatures. With the right selection from the thousands of plants

that are available, a carefully thought out mixed boundary can provide a huge amount of interest for the human, as well as sustaining a diverse range of creatures, which are vital to the food chain and to the pollination of all the plants in the garden.

Below ground, the root systems also play a vital role in the soil structure, both in absorbing and aerating the earth, which is essential for all living things. The leafier a garden is, the better it is for its owner.

If it is chosen carefully, a living boundary can provide a mass of interest, in terms of both colour and fragrance, with flowers and fruits, stems and leaves all contributing to the well-being of humans and wildlife. It can also provide amazing contrast in terms of foliage shapes and structure. Spiky plants can also be useful, to create a deterrent to intruders – a sort of natural barbed wire – and to offer really small garden birds a safe place to nest, eat and live.

An internal boundary or divide is a really good way of segregating a garden, perhaps to separate utility, or the productive part of the garden, from tranquillity – a space to retreat to with a cup of tea and a good book on a summer evening. The internal boundary can help create this separation with minimal work and maximum effect. Working out where the sun will be at certain times of day will allow you to create 'escape rooms' for the siting of a chair or hammock. You do need to remember, however, that the divide will also create shade. I have used internal living divides to separate vegetable plots, to screen off greenhouses and sheds, and to hide a trampoline, where a more tranquil outlook was required. I have seen great success in the use of living divides along inert supports near orchards and vegetable plots, keeping beneficial insects close to plants that need pollination at the correct time, thus ensuring optimum fruit and vegetable production.

Another aim for this book is to explore methods for approaching more difficult boundary situations, such as extending existing hedges or divides and working in restricted environments. A hedge is frequently required for noise reduction or to cover an ugly view. This is often a situation where the most homework is required to get the best long-term results. A plan that is rushed or not properly thought through will ultimately fail. Sometimes, an initial plan may look good on paper and sound ideal, but in practice it will be flawed. It can be particularly difficult to extend existing living boundaries or fill in gaps in them. It can also be challenging to move into a new house and deal with an existing situation, without falling into the trap of making mistakes in terms of plant choice or maintenance. There can even be repercussions when removing an existing boundary and starting all over again, as the pathogens in the ground may be detrimental to the next planting scheme. Hopefully, this book will help you deal with all the challenges involved in creating a living, thriving boundary that contributes to your own well-being and that of your neighbours, and encourages and supports local wildlife.

CHAPTER 1

ASSESSMENT AND PREPARATION

Choosing the plants for your living boundary is probably the most exciting part of the job. However, before you get to that stage, if you want to ensure that you achieve a successful long-term result first time around, you need to undertake a significant amount of assessment and preparation. Forging ahead and relying on good luck goes against the ethos of this book, and the importance of going through the process properly cannot be over-emphasized. Before making any firm decisions, you need to narrow down your options by considering all the different factors that may contribute to the end result. Do not skip this step.

First, it is vital to consider everything that is already there. This includes existing walls and fences, which can themselves be 'greened up' very effectively. If you are going to put in plants close to wall foundations, for example, it is vital that they have the correct type of root system. In a nutshell, a garden designer's vision will only work when the ground work has been done properly. Do not worry if it takes a little bit longer to survey the area and discover the information required to move forward. Remember, the plants you choose now may remain in place for a lifetime or two.

Be wary of being too hasty to get started with the actual planting. Take time to think about and discuss any possible future building works in the garden. There have been examples of a contractor planting a new hedge and then the garden owner deciding to install a patio, and having to dig very close to the establishing roots in order to put in the footings. With better planning and foresight, the footings close to the hedge could be put in place at the time of planting. This action would avoid disturbing the plants as they are establishing themselves. In an ideal world, all hard landscaping (construction) would be finished and out of the way before embarking on the soft landscaping (plants and turf). However, with boundaries this can be tricky as most people prefer to have privacy first, and might want to design the garden around that. Whatever the situation, doing your homework properly will always pay dividends in the long run.

Getting to Know the Existing Environment

Soil Type

Identifying the structure of the soil and its pH is essential as this will help determine which are the right plants for the job and eliminate many of the wrong ones. For example, if you discover that you are dealing with a light, sandy structure with an acidic pH, your list of possible plants will be considerably shortened.

Rhododendrons thrive in acidic soil.

Have a good look around your local area and visit nearby gardens to see what is thriving where. For example, do rhododendrons and azaleas and other acid-loving plants seem to do well in adjacent sites? (Be careful, though, as some gardeners may have gone to great lengths to create an 'acidic bed' for these plants, as the rest of the ground around them would not sustain them.)

Get hold of a soil-testing kit and use it in several places in the area where you are hoping to create a living divide. Once you have an idea of the pH of the soil, it is also well worth digging a sample hole. If necessary, you can do this in several spots along the length of the site. Excavate down a couple of feet and look at the type of soils and stones that emerge. Pour a whole watering can of water into the open sample hole and see if the water escapes quickly or not. This will give a good indication as to how well the soil will hold moisture.

For more on this subject, see Chapters 3 and 4 for detail on various plant species and cultivars.

Location

The geographical location of the site will have a significant influence on your plant choices. Are you planting

Elaeagnus pungens (left) is a shade-tolerant variety, whereas *Elaeagnus ebbingei* (right) prefers a much sunnier location.

within a few miles of the sea or further inland? Locations nearer the sea are warmer than inland in the winter. Salt in the air can also be a big factor, if the garden is really close to the sea – there are many plants that hate salty air, but there are others that love it.

Finding out the average annual temperatures for the location, along with average rainfall, is also helpful in selecting plants, as some are much hardier than others, or more resilient to drought conditions or temporary water-logging. Is the position for the living divide exposed or sheltered? High up or low down? These are all questions that need to be considered if you are to achieve a good result. If there are a number of artificial structures in the garden, or its surroundings, it is worth studying the shade lines as this will have a direct bearing on which cultivars to choose, sometimes even within the same family of plant. Is the land naturally sloping? If so, will the living boundary be on the side of the slope or at the bottom or the top?

The Long-Term Vision

Identifying what you want to achieve from the project is an important part of the process, and should be an integral part that should not be skipped over. Sometimes, you will be tempted by a lovely-looking plant in a pot, buy it on impulse and take it home only to discover that it is wholly unsuitable for the job. If you have a clear long-term vision, this will help you to avoid succumbing to those impulses. This vision should incorporate your choice of colours for foliage and flowers, whether the planting should be evergreen or deciduous (losing its leaves in the winter), and the ultimate height that you want it to reach.

The wrong structure or plants could inhibit rather than help your long-term vision, so you need to ask yourself lots of questions: Do I need this screen as a windbreak, or for privacy or both? What do I want to do with the land around it in the long run? One of the questions that really needs to be answered honestly is: How much knowledge do I have, and how much time will I be able to give over to maintenance? If you have a really busy life and cannot put a maintenance programme together, you will need plants that are forgiving and need very little training. You may be inspired by seeing a feature in a garden that is open to the public, but it is important to remember that many of those gardens have been worked on for several generations. The shape that you see today is probably the result of a huge amount of effort on behalf of a number of gardeners, who have trained the living boundary over many years. Be realistic about your own abilities and the time you will have available.

Remember that the taller the hedge, the bigger the shade line and the bigger the root system. Many a south-facing garden has been cast into shade due to an excessively vigorous hedge or divide at its bottom. The wrong plants, untamed by an inadequate maintenance programme, will also spread width-wise, taking over a significant part of the garden. Without proper planning and plant selection, you may end up with a garden that is half as long and half as wide as it was originally!

An unkempt living boundary (left) compared with a well-maintained one (right).

Plant Selection: Points to Consider

Right Plant, Right Place

Plants come from all corners of the globe and will grow best if you try to emulate their native conditions when planting them in your garden. A happy plant is one that finds itself in an environment where it would naturally try to colonize, as it would have done in the wild. This is one of the reasons why the correct selection process is key to a living boundary that will thrive in the long term. The first stage of this process is mapping out what plants are already at the site, both on your own land and in the neighbours' gardens. Really small shrubs and herbaceous perennials need not be included in this exercise; it is the trees and larger established shrubs that are more likely to have a bearing on what you choose to incorporate in a new living boundary.

A close look at the plant world at this point will give you an understanding of what to plant where. Certain plants do not like being planted within the established root systems of another plant. As a general rule, you should avoid planting another plant in the same family within the confines of the root system of an established one. When you have identified and mapped the existing plants, do some research on the family of each one – this is easily done online. This will give you the next piece of information that you need. Ideally, you want to make sure that your boundary choices do not fit into the families that are already there.

One real-life example that illustrates this theory is that of a laurel hedge *Prunus laurocerasus*, which had been planted in a particular garden by a previous owner. When it was first planted, the hedge had started off nicely and evenly. Three years later, some of the plants had started to slow down, losing vigour and becoming slightly yellow in places, while the other parts had carried on with healthy growth. An inspection revealed that the section of laurel that had gone backwards in performance was running directly over the root system of an established mountain ash tree from next door. The mountain ash or *Sorbus* is related to the laurel – and it was there first. The reason why the laurel had grown so well in the beginning was because it had been planted with a wheelbarrow full of good soil from elsewhere, along with the rest of the hedge. During its establishment phase, it had been using the wheelbarrowed soil, but nearly three years later it had started to grow out of that soil into the root systems of the mountain ash. This was the point when it all started to go wrong. With a bit more homework, such issues might have been averted.

It can be very effective to use an internal hedge both as a windbreak and as a backdrop to flower borders planted in front of it. Holly (*Ilex*) and yew (*Taxus*) are particularly suitable for this use, as they are evergreen, very trainable and dark in colour. The darker the backdrop, the more the plants in front stand out. Of course, it is still important to follow the guidelines of 'right plant, right place'

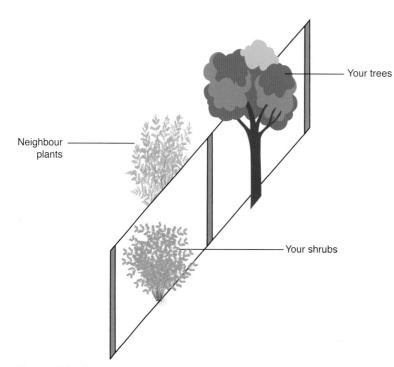

Map and identify what is your neighbours' and what is yours.

Your trees

Neighbour plants

Your shrubs

Green beech (*Fagus sylvatica*).

Barberry (*Berberis*).

Root Systems

It is vitally important to have a knowledge of plant root systems. When something goes wrong above the ground, it is possible to see it and deal with it. If something goes wrong below ground, it can easily go undetected for many years, and can then be very costly to put right. There are many relevant factors relating to root systems, including size and the way they grow. If a living divide is allowed to grow more than it was intended to above ground, the root system below ground will also grow proportionately larger, in order to support the increased weight and counteract the 'sail' effect of the plants in the wind. This means that, even if the hedge is then reduced back to the size that it was first intended to be, it will still have a disproportionately large root system. Every root that grows out from a hedge has an effect on the ground around it. This might mean that the grass in a lawn will suffer, or only certain border plants can be used.

Realizing that the roots of a hedge's plants will have a direct bearing on how the plants are maintained above ground should help you to make your selections wisely.

Hedge planting may also have an impact on nearby infrastructure and buildings, such as walls, patios, driveways, outbuildings, garages, house foundations and underground water systems. For example, a hedge of

An internal hedge of English yew (*Taxus baccata*).

trees, such as beech (*Fagus*), will have a much bigger and wider root system than a hedge of shrubs, such as barberry (*Berberis*). It is very important to be extremely careful when putting in plants with the type of root system that could cause damage in due course. Some plants, for example, have water-seeking roots that will travel far and wide if they find themselves in naturally dry ground. This will create a disproportionately wide-ranging root system, as the roots seek out sufficient moisture. If one of these plants is planted over a drain system that has the smallest of leaks, the roots will colonize at the moisture source and eventually break into the drain and damage the drain system below ground. This will be really expensive to fix, and is completely avoidable with forward planning and homework.

Similarly, there are climbers such as some honeysuckle (*Lonicera*), and wall shrubs such as firethorn (*Pyracantha*), which have moisture roots rather than

Honeysuckle (*Lonicera*) in berry.

Firethorn (*Pyracantha*).

support roots, as they rely on an artificial system to hold them up. Plants with moisture roots only will never grow upwards without some sort of extra support. If a plant with a water-seeking root system is planted in a place where it can find water easily, its roots will not grow out of proportion. Go back to your sample hole – if the ground retains the water, and the spot is away from drains and infrastructure, it may be the right place. For diagrams of various types of root system, *see* Chapters 3 and 4.

Budgeting

When it comes to budgeting for a living boundary, and looking at the cost of plants from a supplier, be aware that the cost will reflect the length of time the plant has been cared for by the nursery. A six-foot plant for the same price as a two-foot one does not necessarily offer better value for money, as both will have taken the same number of years to get to that stage. The price is based on the time that has been devoted to it, the maintenance costs and the materials involved.

There is no such thing as a fast-growing dwarf – if it grows really fast, then it would want to be very large if left alone. This would indicate that, if you wanted to keep it small, it would need to be pruned very often. Just think carefully, as you are not pruning the roots below ground from day one of being planted in the final growing place. If you find that you have narrowed it down to a couple of choices of plants suitable for the screen you are looking for, the choice should reflect your maintenance level.

If the budget is fairly tight, it is better to spend more on preparation and buy smaller plants than the other way round. Do not sacrifice pre-planting work on the soil in order to buy bigger, more expensive plants. Good preparation will help the roots on the new plants to establish very quickly and easily. The tops will develop more quickly and be less stressed than those on a plant that is struggling due to the lack of preparation. When plants are stressed they are less likely to fight off disease and do not establish easily. Plants – both evergreen and deciduous – sometimes go into premature dormancy after being planted, throwing all their leaves off and waiting for their roots to find the right balance below ground. Once this has been achieved, hopefully they will then shoot out again above ground, with new foliage. Sometimes, natural die-back will occur, and the plant will then produce new leaves on healthy wood below the area of dieback.

Getting it Right First Time

The time and money you invest in planting and maintaining your living boundary will be well spent, as long as you do your homework and make the right choices about which plants will be suitable. If you get it right first time, you should not have to revisit the issue ever again. The aim is to plant a hedge or living divide once, get it right, and then enjoy watching it get better and better with age. There are plenty of pitfalls in the world of garden design and it is such a shame if the wrong plant is used, time goes by and the result is wrong for the garden owner – and for their neighbour. Sometimes, maintenance becomes an issue because the plants were not right for the job in the first place, and the hedge then becomes an eyesore or nuisance. In extreme cases, the owner may even end up pulling it out and starting all over again. At that point, future options for a second round of planting in the same place will definitely be limited. When old plants are removed, often the soil that is left behind, where all the roots have travelled down, will have lost its necessary balance of nutrients.

Before starting any work, you should determine whether you need to notify the authorities. Many border plants and trees come under the regulation of the local council, as they tend to be longer-lived than other features in a garden, so it is important it is to be thorough at this stage.

If you are acting as a contractor, it is really important to give the customer thorough and appropriate advice. They may have seen and liked a feature elsewhere and try to insist on having it in their own garden, but it may well be wrong for the situation and conditions, and demand too high a level of maintenance – to say nothing of the other long-term requirements. For the private dwelling, a well-kept boundary will always add value in the eyes of a potential buyer, compared to one that has been allowed to get out of hand. There is a sense of peace that the boundaries are all in order, and the new owners can simply carry on the maintenance that the previous owner has been doing so well over their tenure. The story can be quite different when borders have been left to become unruly, leading to neighbourly disputes and sometimes even authorities getting involved. Sometimes, paying somebody to maintain a hedge will offer the best value for money in the long run, compared to letting things get out of hand and then trying to bring them back, which will be time-consuming, messy and costly.

CHAPTER 2

DESIGN AND PLANNING

Note: each of the sub-sections of this chapter should be helpful when approaching the design of a boundary, and it is probably wise to read all of it before venturing into the nitty gritty of which plant varieties to choose. This should give you an awareness of the situations you may encounter and, particularly, of the pitfalls. Remember that plants on your boundary will be there for a long time, so if it takes a little longer to understand a particular situation and address it correctly, it will be worth it.

The fedge and mound sections cover the situations in which those features can be used for the best results, with diagrams for illustration. The hypotenuse section identifies a way of blocking views without creating unnecessary shade lines, again with diagrams to help

you calculate the correct measurements. It is important to be strategic with shade – too often, gardens suffer from excessive shade, generally as a result of poor plant selection and inadequate levels of maintenance. Most garden owners, especially in the UK, will want to be able to enjoy a bit of sunshine.

Fedges: How and When to Use Them

There are two different types of fedge: one incorporates living plants, such as willow (*Salix*), using the woody part as the fence and the leafy part as the hedge. These can be quite ornamental if trained

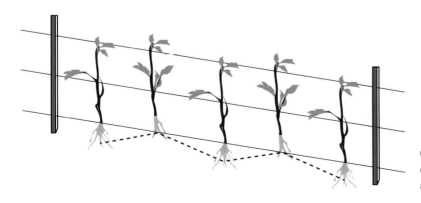

Creating a fedge: planting on opposite sides of a fence to create a subtle zig-zag.

When planting on the alternate side of a wire fence to make a fedge, ideally use a more open style rather than chicken wire.

A fedge created from a mixed living boundary grown through a post and rail fence.

Planting on alternate sides of a post and rail fence to make a fedge.

correctly. The second type is a cross between a fence and a hedge and this is the focus here. It usually comprises a basic fence in the middle of the divide – a simple wooden post and wire, or wooden post and wooden rail, or wooden post with animal-proof wire – planted up with shrubs or young trees, alternating on either side of it. For this method to work, new growth on the plants should be tied in to the fence using natural garden string or jute, which will rot and fall off within a year or so, allowing the plants to grow on uninhibited once they are strong enough. As long as the new growth is regularly tied in during the main growing season, eventually the shrubs will hide the fence part completely. If the fedge incorporates animal-proof wire, it will also allow a dog to be kept in the garden from day one. This type of fedge will just look like a normal hedge once it is mature. Over the very long term, the timber of the fence part may rot away and disappear, leaving behind the living part.

A fedge may be suitable for a number of situations:

- Where there is a need for a hedge to become really dense and narrow and stay that way.
- A fedge can create a divide that no one can walk through right from the date of planting. This one is often used on the edges of open areas that are accessible to the public, where unwanted visitors are more likely to walk through the new planting. It is also a good way to protect a front garden from the pavement, to prevent post office workers and delivery people taking the shortest route to the front door. Planting a hedge rather than a fedge runs the risk of a gap forming in the boundary as it grows, due to damage while it is young.
- In a very exposed position, this technique will help a living divide with support and protection while it is young, allowing it to develop a strong base while it is establishing its root system.
- Over a few years, spiky plants such as firethorn (*Pyracantha*) – nature's barbed wire – can be used to create an impenetrable divide. The new growth is

very flexible, with softer spikes, so it will need to be tied in regularly to the fence, using jute or natural string. Eventually, the fedge will be impossible to walk through or climb over, and will provide food and shelter for birds and wildlife.

- The fedge can be built to the exact size and length of boundary that is required in the long run, giving a framework for gardeners and future contractors to work to. This type of living divide can be quite tall.
- A fedge is ideal for growing climbing plants through, as the fence part will provide instant support and useful tying-in points, while the shrubs or young trees for the hedge part are establishing. This is very effective for the first three years, as it will take a while for the hedge part to develop sufficiently to act as a support for the climbing plants. The other advantage is that the roots will not yet have established fully on the hedge, so the climbers can be planted without fighting its root systems. Adding climbing plants later could potentially damage the roots of the hedge. The most suitable climbers for this are roses and clematis. Vigorous woody climbers such as wisteria will try to twine on wire, which can kill the section of the woody climber several years down the line, as well as fighting the hedge plants in the long run. Use clematis plants from pruning Group Three, such as *Clematis viticella* types, which will grow through the framework of the fedge every year and flower on the outside of it in late summer. This works well on evergreens, but not conifers. During the winter the clematis will have no leaves and very little structure, if you have used the correct varieties. In the second week of February, its stems should be severed a couple of feet off the ground and the stems above that left to disintegrate. The *Clematis viticella* species has a wide range of varieties and colours, including whites, blues, pinks, burgundies and mauves. They are capable of attaining a height of eight to ten feet through the fedge every year on an established root.
- A fedge can create a tangible boundary to a certain size, for example, to meet regulations from day one. However, it also offers the opportunity to display a fabulous twist to its long-term appearance, with the fence part being adorned to great effect with annual climbers such as Black-Eyed Susan and nasturtiums while the hedge part is getting going. These may be smaller plants but they still produce a fabulous

result. A one-sided fedge can make an effective internal divide between a garden and a vegetable plot. The fence can provide support for blackberry or tayberry plants, for example, on the vegetable and fruit side, while the garden side can be the ornamental living divide, using stand-alone shrubs. If animal-proof wire is used, that can be very effective at keeping marauding species out of the fruit and vegetable area from day one. The other significant benefit is that it will provide shelter for over-wintering insects, very close to where they will be needed for pollination purposes on the edible crops. One good example is the hoverfly, which acts as a pollinator for early fruit trees, particularly the pear. (Incidentally, horticulturalists usually advise that pear trees should be positioned on the west side of other trees, so that the sun does not damage dew-laden blossom in the spring. The sun reaches the pear later in the day, when the flowers have dried up, and it can no longer damage them.) Pollinators also appreciate lots of woody structure, where they can shelter while they are waking up for spring.

In a nutshell, the fedge is a space-saving, shaped screening feature that has many uses and is easy to maintain for the regular gardener.

Mounds: How to Use Them

Mounds, or bunds, as they are called in the trade, have a wide range of uses. In basic terms, a bund is an area of raised ground, sometimes created with imported soil. When it comes to boundaries, the bunding method is very useful in a number of situations:

Example 1

A bund can keep vehicles out, but still allow the garden owner to enjoy the view. Often a digger is required for this type of bunding, as a ditch is dug on the inside of the land and the spoil from the ditch becomes the bund. The bund can be planted up very effectively with small plants that provide lots of colour and softening, but never get tall, so that they do not block the view. Too often, a boundary system will obscure a lovely view, when the aim is simply to hide just one unsightly feature somewhere along the length of the divide.

An empty boundary bund or mound, which could be planted up.

A planted hedge on a bund.

Example 2

Where the soil is prone to waterlogging in the winter, or for long periods of time after heavy rain, a bunding method can allow the use of a much wider range of boundary plants. Planting directly into heavy ground is always problematic, as it creates a sump effect, with the hole filling up after rain. Very few plants like to have a waterlogged root system. The bunding method can resolve this, as the plants will be elevated on the mound and their root systems will be aerated all year round.

An open bund or mound – planting optional.

Example 3

A bund can provide an instant boundary, which can be planted up or can be left to naturalize. If you decide to plant along the ridge of the bund, the slope side of the mound that is visible from the house can be very effectively planted up with low-growing herbaceous perennials. This will provide colour at the base of the ridge planting and will give a good level of interest all year round, but will require very little maintenance.

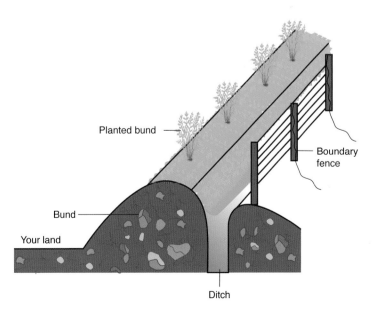

Planted bund

Boundary fence

Bund

Your land

Ditch

Bund Example 1 – one option.

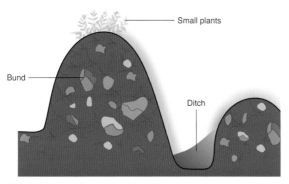

Bund Example 1 – a second option.

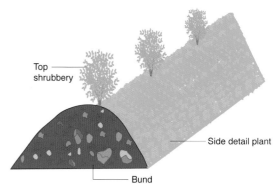

Bund Example 3.

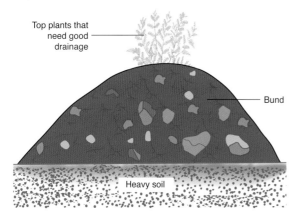

Bund Example 2.

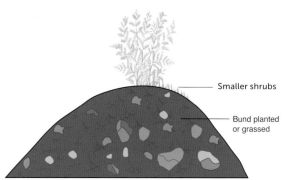

Bund Example 4.

Example 4

Generally, the average boundary only needs to be around six feet high. A mound or bund can provide part of that height, and a very effective boundary can then be created with much smaller shrubs, rather than the more vigorous plants, which require more pruning and looking after.

Example 5

Existing post and rail or wire fencing can be half buried by a bund, allowing the under-planting of the fence in a very effective way. When the sloping side is planted up, the feature is called badging. Basically, it can bring detail plants to the foreground, so that they can be seen well from a distance. If such plants are planted on the flat, the viewer has to approach closer in order to see them properly.

Example 6

Where a garden is fortunate enough to have very rich soil, a bund can provide a good opportunity to grow those plants that prefer poorer conditions. The soil of the bund will only get poorer as its nutrients are washed out over time, but certain plants will appreciate such an impoverished environment. Emulating nature is always important if plants are to grow properly to their correct proportions, and thrive. One of the problems in the UK is that plants grow too big because the soil is too rich in comparison with their native habitat. This creates a disproportionately large plant that will flower less and less as time goes on. Planting on the impoverished soil of a bund will restrict growth and therefore enhance the flowering ability of plants such as rosemary (*Rosmarinus*) and butterfly bush (*Buddleja*).

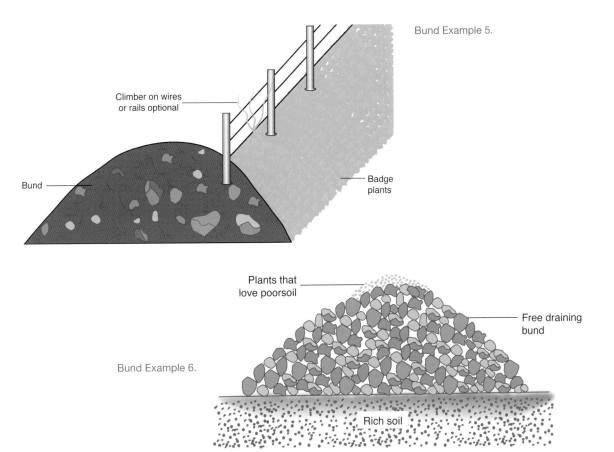

Bund Example 5.

Climber on wires or rails optional

Bund

Badge plants

Plants that love poorsoil

Free draining bund

Bund Example 6.

Rich soil

Example 7

An existing low wall could be backed with soil on one side, and the top planted up, creating a half mound or bund. This could enable you to plant tumbling plants at the top of the wall to soften it as they grow down-wards. Before creating such a feature, it is vital to get the existing wall professionally checked and, if neces-sary, strengthened, in order to cope with the load. If the wall is not strong enough to bear the extra weight, the whole thing may crack apart or even collapse completely, making it rather dangerous. If there is no suitable existing wall, it is possible to create the fea-ture from scratch, building a wall that is fit for pur-pose. In this case, there are other ways of retaining the front of the bund – rather than a stone or brick wall, railway sleepers or rough rocks could be used. The same principle applies in terms of ensuring that the retaining structure is strong enough to hold the weight of the soil behind and the plants above. Do not

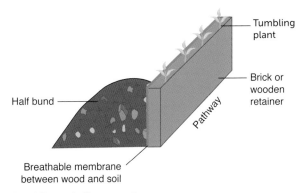

Tumbling plant

Brick or wooden retainer

Half bund

Pathway

Breathable membrane between wood and soil

Bund Example 7 – one option.

plant anything above a wall that will grow too large, such as a plant from the tree world, as in time its root systems will create too much pressure on the struc-ture below.

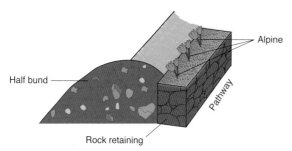

Bund Example 7 – a second option.

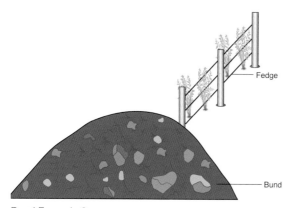

Bund Example 8.

An effective internal hedge of English Yew (*Taxus baccata*).

Example 8

This last option – a combination of fedge and mound – might just be the best, providing huge benefits for the garden owner, for wildlife and for any neighbours. It will incorporate a badged base for detailed plants up to a small fence and hedge, which will allow a diverse range of plants and a structure for wildlife. In order to achieve colour and interest all year round, plant winter interest plants on the badged part, particularly if that part of the garden can be seen from the house during those months that are so often lacking in colour.

The Internal Living Boundary

An internal hedge is ideal for separating the ornamental part of a garden from a vegetable plot, but this is not the only option for this type of boundary. There are several situations where a living internal divide could be of benefit:

- Perhaps the most obvious use is to hide a shed, garage or outbuilding. The benefit of this is that the

An internal hedge outlining a pathway.

outdoor space will appear more green from a distance instead of there being a man-made structure in full view, but at the same time the living divide will be separate from the structure, and will therefore be less likely to cause damage to its woodwork or brickwork.

- A living divide can be used to provide privacy or a peaceful outlook, surrounding a space for the

An effective internal living divide, using stand-alone trellis and climbing plants.

garden owner to sit and relax, or entertain, perhaps around a patio or less formal space.

- In a very exposed garden, a series of living divides can act as a windbreak, slowing down the wind sufficiently to allow delicate planting in pockets. If they are positioned with care, living divides within a windy space can also provide some lovely places to sit and catch the sun without being blown around.
- Internal hedges or living divides can add more natural habitats for all sorts of wildlife across a property, helping to redress the wildlife deficit from urban spaces, caused by increased infrastructure. Pollinators can also be brought closer to the flower borders.
- If the land is stepped, an internal divide can denote the edge of the steps and help stop someone falling in the area. Its root systems can also help hold the land together. It can be planted either at the top or bottom of the step, creating a natural edge to the feature.
- Many gardens have play or working areas that contain unsightly items, such trampolines, parked wheelbarrows, storage areas, and so on. These can all be hidden away from the ornamental part of the garden by an internal hedge, helping that part of the garden to stay tranquil.
- An internal divide can be very useful as a backdrop to flower borders. If the backdrop incorporates a combination of man-made support and climbing plants, it is possible to achieve flowering interest over a very long period of time. There are many climbing plants that will flower for months. Planting the foreground border with plants that will contrast in colour with the backdrop will add interest.
- A mixed internal living divide, with a combination of flowering and fruiting shrubs in a row, can also provide ingredients for cooking and preserving. This type of hedge works well to divide or encompass a vegetable plot. Determine the varieties that you know you will use and plant several of the same variety. Typical hedgerow jams or jellies might use a combination of the following: elderberry (*Sambucus nigra*), sloe (*Prunus spinosa*), damson (*Prunus domestica Insititia*), myrobalan, or cherry plum (*Prunus ceracifera*), hawthorn (*Crataegus laevigata*), blackberry (*Rubus*), crab apples (*Malus sylvestris*), rowan (*Sorbus aucuparia*), raspberry (*Rubus idaeus*). Rosehips are also useful. They are produced on a host of wild and shrub roses. The most widely used, because they are available in bare-root form, are the *Rosa rugosa* varieties, but there are many more. Some of these become pretty sparse in the winter months, so this type of planting may not be the answer where a view needs to be blocked all year round.

Generally, an internal divide does not need to be as dense as an outer living boundary, or to hold its structure all year round, as might be expected from an outer boundary.

Using the Hypotenuse

Many gardens have something fairly unsightly in view, and it is also extremely unusual for a garden not to be overlooked from any direction. The technique of using the hypotenuse can help you achieve more of a feeling of your land being just for you and for the nature around you, especially if you are less fortunate

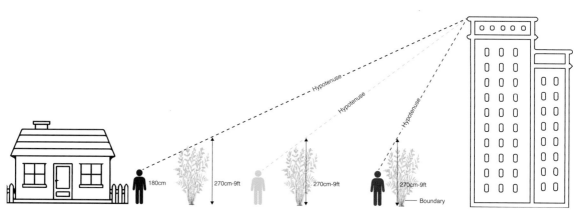

Hypotenuse

Foreground
planting
whilst hedge
is developing

180cm-6ft

270cm-9ft

Final
hedge
height

427cm-14ft

Use hypotenuse calculations to allow you to grow slower hedges for less maintenance.

Hypotenuse

Hypotenuse

Hypotenuse

180cm

270cm-9ft

270cm-9ft

270cm-9ft

Boundary

Use the hypotenuse to create strategic islands, keeping eyesores beyond your boundary out of sight, whilst still allowing maximum light into your garden.

in these respects. If you have an annoying view from a particular window or place where you sit in the garden, or perhaps you are overlooked from a particular vantage point, using the hypotenuse will save you from boundary heartache, in both the short term and the long run.

The first instinct of most garden owners is to go to the edge of their land and plant the biggest, fastest-growing living divide they can. However, this is potentially a mistake and may be fraught with issues. Remember, you need to cohabit peacefully with your neighbours. The closer your planting is to the object

An island in the foreground, softening the view of the higher house behind.

that you are trying to hide, the larger the screen needs to be if it is to be successful. Using the hypotenuse technique can help you to follow a different path.

As an example, imagine a satellite dish on the roof of your neighbour's house, which spoils the lovely view that you can see when you sit on your patio. Using the hypotenuse trick, you can 'remove' the satellite dish, but at the same time you can keep the rest of the lovely view around it. This can be done by using the foreground, nearer to your seating area, and creating a much smaller planting scheme with plants that will grow to just above your head height. In order to hide the satellite dish, the foreground planting scheme does not need to be very wide either. This is effectively touching the hypotenuse to remove the vantage point (the unsightly object) from view.

Similarly, the hypotenuse can be exploited by those who are fortunate enough to have quite a long or wide garden, in creating a series of planted islands at the correct distancing. The island plantings may be only a few inches taller than the average person, but they will prevent parts of the garden being overlooked, and will also screen certain items that you may not want to see.

The technique may also be used in the creation of a temporary raised planting scheme in tubs and troughs, near to the house or seating area, which will break your eyeline from day one. A slower hedge can then be planted in the distance, on the boundary. This will require a lot less work in the long run once it is established and, being slower-growing, will generally end up in a much more manageable result.

Clearly, the hypotenuse method allows you to plant the correct living divide first time around. It should avoid the need for fast-growing plants on your boundary. You can even start small with the plants, as long as your preparation is thorough (*see* Chapter 5 for more on planting methods).

This planted island creates manageable height in the foreground.

CHAPTER 3

HEDGING PLANTS

Shrubs

The shrub selection available to gardeners is huge and this list is by no means exhaustive. There is nothing stopping you putting different plants together to form a divide, but you need to bear in mind that different plants will have different growth rates, which may result in an uneven finish. Additionally, some shrubs are much shorter-lived than others. Plant growth rates may also vary depending on the growing conditions – the colder and more exposed the location, the slower

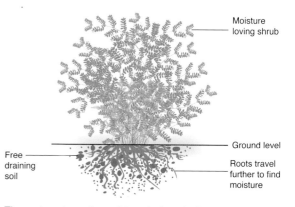

The root system of a moisture-loving shrub.

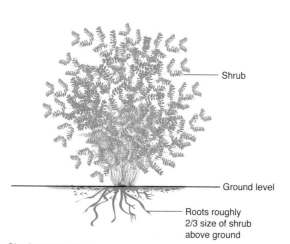

Shrub root system.

and smaller the growth, compared with the same plants over the same period of time in a warmer, more sheltered environment.

Berberis (Barberry)

There are many fabulous barberry varieties, which provide great habitats for wildlife, as well as offering security against intruders and beauty for much of the year. Some are evergreen and some are deciduous; all are spiky. Many of them flower profusely as well as fruiting abundantly, providing food for garden birds.

Key

S	Small	Will grow less than 90cm (3ft) in ten years; easy to maintain as a low living divide
M	Medium	Capable of 1.25–2.5m (4–8ft) in ten years, but could be kept clipped between one and two feet less, as a living divide
L	Large	Will grow above 2.75m (9ft) in ten years, but could be kept to three feet less as a living divide
SU	Sunny position	
SH	Shady position	
SUSH	Both sun and shade	
W	Wet and heavy soils	
D	Dry and stony or sandy soils, or planted on mounds above heavy and wetter soils	
AC	Acidic to neutral soils	
AL	Alkaline soils	
ACAL	All soils	
EV	Evergreen	
DE	Deciduous	

Berberis candidula.

The family is Berberidaceae, and it is related to *Mahonia*, among others. Not much attacks a barberry, apart from occasional rust, and it generally stays looking good if the growing conditions are right. A waterlogged soil is probably its least favourite environment.

Berberis candidula
S, SUSH, D, ACAL, EV

A rather under-used plant, with small pointed leaves, silvery beneath and glossy green above. Capable of 90cm (3ft). Very reliable and impenetrable, once established.

Berberis darwinii
M, SUSH, D, ACAL, EV

A valuable evergreen cultivar that will produce a nice six-foot hedge in a ten-year period, but is capable of more than twice that in the long term, if left to its own devices. It will look quite enviable at between four and six foot. Space them 45cm (18in) apart from 3-litre pots when planting. As a stand-alone shrub it has an arched habit, producing masses of orange flowers in the spring and purple/blue fruits in the winter, the birds love it. It is great on impoverished soils and is hardy for inland planting as well as doing well near the sea, but it must not be planted where the ground is liable to become waterlogged. It prefers sandy, stony ground or even an old building site to a non-aerated, heavy soil

Berberis darwinii.

Berberis darwinii 'Compacta'.

that holds too much water. It is excellent planted on a bund or mound. It is completely happy on acidic and alkaline soils, and in both sun or semi-shade.

Berberis darwinii 'Compacta'
S, SUSH, D, ACAL, EV

A miniature version of *Berberis darwinii*, with all the same features, but leaves, flowers and fruits that are quite a bit smaller, and a tighter habit. It can reach five feet, but if it is kept at three feet or so, it will make a wonderful divide between areas of the garden and under windows, to deter intruders. Space them about 30–40cm (15in) apart when planting them as a small hedge.

Berberis gagnepainii
M, SUSH, D, ACAL, EV

This cultivar is capable of growing to eight feet but very slow to get there, so it is ideal for a four- to six-foot hedge, if it is going to be pruned. Like an evergreen

Berberis gagnepainii.

with a difference, it has green leaves during the summer, which turn bright red on exposed plants when the weather gets cold, then drop off in the spring as the new green leaves appear. As a result, there is plenty of interest on top of the mid-yellow flowers in the spring and bluey fruits in the winter. It probably deserves to be grown more widely, although it is not good for an exterior boundary, unless it is on a mound, as it is probably too slow from ground level. It makes a fabulous internal boundary, though. Space the plants 45cm (18in) apart when planting for a hedge. As it is naturally arching, some people incorporate it in a fedge, tying it in to the fence with jute, to keep it more upright. It is at home in acidic and alkaline soils, and sun and shade. It makes an excellent stand-alone variety too.

Berberis × media 'Red Jewel'
S, SU and semi SH, D, ACAL, semi EV

This beautiful compact form is very spiky, so you will need to wear gloves when handling it. It works well as an edging plant, regularly clipped to create a small two-foot high and one-foot wide hedge. It is burgundy during the growing season, and in winter it will lose most, but not all, of its leaves, then regenerate them all again in the spring. The colour is a fabulous contrast to other foliage colours in the garden. In spring it produces yellow flowers, often as the new leaves are starting. In the autumn it has occasional red fruits. It is good in soils that are poor, both alkaline and acidic, and is better in open spaces rather than under trees in heavy shade. Good drainage is important for a happy hedge. Spacing should be about 30–40cm (15in).

Berberis stenophylla
M, SUSH, D, ACAL, EV.

This variety looks rather wiry and sparse in a 3-litre pot, but once it is in open ground, it takes on a whole new dimension. It is naturally scandent, or lax, in habit, and will make best progress in the short term if it is tied in with jute to a simple fence through the middle of a hedge, or fedge (*see* Chapter 2). When it is growing under the fedge system to start with, it is very easy to keep this plant only a couple of feet wide and eight feet tall, making it a valuable living divide. It is happy in sun and semi-shade. It thrives on poor soils as long as they are free-draining. Once the roots have established, it may achieve as much as 45cm (18in) a year. On the fedge system, it will be more impressive more quickly, but this will require more maintenance work in the early years. This variety may be staggered on either side of the fence at 40–45cm (15–18in) spacing to create the fedge.

Berberis × media 'Red Jewel'.

Berberis stenophylla.

Berberis thunbergii.

Berberis thunbergii 'Atropurpurea' – purple foliage.

Berberis thunbergii
M, SU, D, ACAL, DE

Yellow-flowered and with pale green foliage, this deciduous variety loves well-drained, poor soils and sunny situations. Producing teardrop-shaped red fruits in the autumn in profusion, it is wonderful for wildlife all year round. It is very hardy and is great in an open position, but it will not thrive if it is planted in the shade. The best divides of this variety are five or so feet high and can be kept pretty narrow. It can sometimes be found with bare-root mixed hedging in the winter in the UK. It is most often used in a mixed hedge, but it can also be used as a single cultivar hedge, in which case spacing of 40–45cm (15–18in) is fine. If you want to mix it with *Berberis thunbergii atropurpurea* (*see* below), plant two burgundy ones to one green one, as the burgundy variety is less vigorous.

Berberis thunbergii atropurpurea
S–M, SU, D, ACAL, DE

This variety is similar to *Berberis thunbergii*, but slightly slower to get to size, and with strong burgundy foliage. It is great at creating contrast with other plants and very attractive during the season, but it does lose its leaves in the winter, so you need to consider your circumstances carefully in order to use it effectively. Will it still provide enough privacy during the dormant months? The deciduous varieties are generally faster than the evergreens in their initial growth while young. Spacing of about 40cm (15in) is right for this variety.

Buxus (Box)

Box is related to a wonderful ground-cover plant called *Pachysandra* and a very fragrant winter shrub called *Sarcococca*. The family is known as Buxaceae and its varieties all need good drainage at their feet; waterlogging is probably the worst issue for this plant. The other thing box plants hate is root disturbance, so they should always be positioned in a spot that will not have to be dug once they have been planted. When using box, the layout of the garden must be right first time, especially if there is a plan to incorporate a path or walkway, either straight away or at some time in the future. Once the roots of the box shrubs are established, you do not want to go and cut holes in the hedge, for example, to sink a paving slab. Doing this would lead to an increased risk of the plants near the hole either dying or contracting box blight, which would cause significant problems. Horticulture students are usually taught to give box its first trim on the Ides of March (the 15th) and its second towards the end of June. It should never be trimmed in the autumn or winter. For best results, use container-grown plants. Box is often sold in 2-litre pots for the larger forms, which are very slow, and in 1-litre pots for the smaller forms, which are even slower. If you buy them as bare-root or field-grown plants, you will need to containerize them for a year before planting them out into a hedge. This way, any that do not survive will still be in their pot rather than in a living divide situation.

Buxus sempervirens
S, SU, D, ACAL, EV

This variety of box is wonderful for positions in sun and light shade, spaced about 30cm (12in) apart, when planted as a small hedge, in well-drained soil. It is ideal for a narrow divide along a pathway, and best kept to around one to two feet in height. It is slow-growing, so plants should not be spaced any more than 30cm (12in) apart, otherwise it will not make an uninterrupted small hedge – there will always be gaps in it. Large topiary features in clipped box will certainly be very old, as it will take many years to reach such a size, and it is very long-lived.

Buxus sempervirens.

Buxus sempervirens 'Suffruticosa'
S, SU, D, ACAL, EV

This is a very slow form, so it should be spaced no more than 15cm (6in) apart when planting. Good drainage is essential for this very slow form. Often sold in 9cm and 1 litre pots. You would expect this to really be neatly clipped six inch in height and spread, a small running square, evergreen sausage growing around a detailed garden situation, such as an alpine garden. This is not suitable for topiary. You only need on cut per year in March.

Ceanothus

See 'Wall Shrubs'.

Chamaecyparis Lawsoniana

See 'Conifers'.

Cornus (Dogwood)
M, SU, W, ACAL, DE

The *Cornus* (dogwood) world is big, and there are a few that are appropriate for planting in a living divide. They are often sold in bare-foot form in the winter. The *Cornus alba* types are brilliant plants for moist ground and exposure. During the summer this dogwood is leafy. If it is pruned hard at the end of January each year, almost back to ground level, the stems will colour up in the winter, after the leaves have fallen off. It can grow back to 1.5–1.8m (5–6ft) in a season, but the drawback is that, if you need the plants as a permanent living boundary, at a decent height like this, you will not get the vibrant winter stems. If they are pruned only lightly, the stems will not colour up, apart from at the very top of the plant. Meanwhile, it will produce lots of white flowers in the spring and white fruits that often go bluey in the winter. Alternatives include yellow-stemmed varieties such as *Cornus stolonifera* 'Flaviramea' and *C. alba* 'Kesselringii', which has black stems in winter. There are many other forms, most of which are available to buy in containers.

Corylus (Hazel)

Generally supplied as bare-root plants in the winter, the hazel family offers many ornamental forms as well

Variegated *Cornus alba*.

Cornus alba 'Kesselringii'.

Cornus stolonifera 'Flaviramea'.

as edible ones. For the purpose of living divides, the two below are particularly good – one with burgundy foliage and one with green foliage. These are best in semi-shade; in hot summers, the foliage can become quite scorched in direct sun.

Corylus avellana (Hazelnut)
M, SH, W, ACAL, DE

Usually, hazels are sold as mixed hedging in bare-root form in the winter. They are available from nurseries and other suppliers as bare-root whips in various heights, from 40–60cm (16–24in) to 60–80cm (24–32in), and so on. They have yellow winter catkins and may produce hazelnuts in the autumn if sufficient numbers are planted near each other, as they would be in a coppice of hazel in a woodland, ensuring adequate pollination. If they are planted sporadically in a mixed hedge, they will usually just produce the yellow catkins and not much in the way of nuts. They are excellent for shady locations and can be cut back very hard at the end of winter, resprouting from the base. The cut sticks

Corylus avellana.

Corylus maxima 'Purpurea'.

Corylus avellana with developing fruit.

are often used by allotment gardeners to support peas and beans. Hazel lends itself well to the technique of layering.

Corylus maxima 'Purpurea'

M, semi SH, W, ACAL, DE.

This variety has a much larger leaf. It is burgundy in colour, with grey catkins in the winter, and it provides excellent contrast in a mixed hedge.

Cotoneaster

There are hundreds of varieties of *Cotoneaster*. As they are all related to the rose (in the Rosaceae family), it is important to be careful not to plant them too close to the established root systems of other plants also related to the rose. For example, a cotoneaster will really struggle if it is planted across the root system of a pre-existing mountain ash, and will fail to thrive where the roots meet each other. If, however, you are planting on an untouched patch of ground, you can put in a number of members of the rose plant family together, as long as you plant them all at the same time. They should all thrive, as none of them will have been established earlier than any others. If you are planting into a seemingly open patch of ground, it is worth finding out what may have been growing there previously. There may be nothing obvious on the surface, but remnants of old planting may lurk under the ground and will interfere with the new. One classic situation is where an old orchard has fallen into disuse, the fruit trees have been removed and the area has been turfed over, and left alone. As many fruit trees are also related to the rose, that ground will still not sustain a Rosaceae hedge well, even up to ten or fifteen years later. Rose sickness and lack of nutrition may affect the next roseaceous member (for example, a cotoneaster) and prevent it thriving.

There is a good reason why apples are round – it is so that they can roll away from the parent in order to germinate and create a new tree far enough away from the existing root system. You will never find a new apple tree growing up over the root system of the parent tree. If there is a small apple tree growing up underneath a bigger one, it will be a shoot from the existing root system.

All cotoneasters can suffer from blight and other problems that commonly affect members of the rose family, such as blackspot and sometimes mildews. However, the varieties listed below are generally pretty bullet-proof, although they are not especially long-lived. It is unusual to find one over fifty years old that is really healthy and it is usually the older ones that show signs of these illnesses. In terms of geographical location, it is not uncommon to see groups of cotoneasters doing really well within a mile of the sea, as well as inland. They do seem to hold their leaves better when they are nearer the sea, or in milder locations during the winter.

Cotoneaster cornubia
L, SUSH, D, ACAL, semi EV

Because this variety has vigour, and is almost evergreen, it is probably the most versatile in the *Cotoneaster* world. It can be grown against a fence, in sun and shade. It has a rather lax habit, so the narrowest ones will need to be tied with jute on to something, such as support wires, bamboo canes, trellis, and so on. It lends itself very well to being trained as a fedge, which will

Cotoneaster cornubia.

give plenty of tying-in points while the plant is young. It is sometimes sold as a tree, as well as a shrub. It is capable of attaining 4.5m (15ft) in height, but it can be controlled to make an excellent divide 2.5–2.75m (8–9ft) high, and can be kept very narrow if it is given support. With its multitude of white flowers in the spring, and masses of red berries in the autumn, it is much loved by insects and birds. Because the new growth is whippy, it must not be left unsupported, as it will begin to droop, but it does lend itself well to training and pleaching (*see* Chapter 5). If the plants are spaced at three-foot intervals against a support, they will soon fill in.

Cotoneaster exburiensis
M–L, SUSH, D, ACAL, semi EV

This form is slightly less vigorous than *C. cornubia*, but it is still capable of attaining over twelve feet or so. It holds fewer leaves, and has creamy yellow berries in the autumn, making it a great source of feed for birds later in the season. It is lax in habit and therefore requires

Cotoneaster exburiensis.

Cotoneaster franchetii in flower.

support, if it is required to be in a formal shape. It can be bought as a tree or as a shrub, and the plants can be spaced 60–90cm (2–3ft) apart quite comfortably against the support, where it can be tied in and trained. It is a good variety for growing as a fedge or for pleaching.

Cotoneaster franchettii
M, SUSH, D, ACAL, EV

This is probably one of the most resilient forms of *Cotoneaster*. Capable of reaching eight feet, it has an arching habit, orangey-red berries, and a silver under-side to an evergreen leaf. It thrives on the poorest ground of all, and it readily self-seeds. Because of its lax habit, it requires some tying in if it is to be kept nice and narrow. It has many stems to its base; with age, this makes it very thick low down in the hedge. It works very well in a mixed hedge as a nice splash of almost evergreen among the generally deciduous varieties. The plants should be spaced 60cm (2ft) apart when being planted as a hedge. An excellent roadside plant.

Cotoneaster *franchetii* with fruit.

Cotoneaster horizontalis
S–M, SUSH, D, ACAL, DE

Also known as the herringbone cotoneaster, this wonderful variety has branches that can be grown

Cotoneaster horizontalis.

Cotoneaster lacteus.

nicely against a shaded wall or fence. It is deciduous, with rich red autumn colour and vibrant red berries, and white flowers in spring. It is excellent for a small hedge of three feet high or less, with a small support, and up to six feet, given time, against a bigger structure such as a trellis. The birds and the bees love this plant. The plants should be spaced 60cm (2ft).

C. *horizontalis* 'Variegatus' is a superb, very striking variegated variety of the herringbone cotoneaster that is less vigorous

Cotoneaster lacteus
M, SUSH, D, ACAL, EV

This variety produces red berries profusely and has masses of white flowers in the spring. The foliage is evergreen and the plant is capable of reaching a height of six feet. It is very lax in habit, requiring plenty of support against trellising, but it is worth the extra tying in, using Jute. Due to its lax form, the plants should be spaced 60–90cm (2–3ft) apart.

Cotoneaster microphyllus
S, SUSH, D, ACAL, EV

This very compact, small-leafed evergreen has berries that appear to be pinkish in the autumn, but become redder as the winter progresses, as well as white flowers in the spring. Due to its robust nature, this form is often used in municipal settings, as it makes an almost impenetrable two- to three-feet high and two- to three-feet wide divide, which can run alongside a pathway and

Cotoneaster microphyllus.

withstand all sorts of treatment from the public. When planted as a hedge, spacing of 45cm (18in) is fine. This cotoneaster is excellent for wildlife, as it is incredibly thick when it is established, creating a safe and secure habitat where creatures can hide and thrive.

Crataegus (Hawthorn)

All of the hawthorns are in the Rosaceae family, related to the rose, so they need to be planted in previously untouched ground, or in a place where there are no remnants of other members of that family. They require a similar sort of preparation to *Cotoneaster*. They are available in many forms as a tree (*see* also 'Hedge Trees' in Chapter 7), including field-grown whips, which may be purchased and planted during the winter months. They are tough and will thrive in exposed situations. Really, the only issues that affect them are mildews and rusts, which can occur while they are establishing, and particularly when they have been planted in a spot that is too sheltered or over-protected. They also dislike waterlogged soils when young, but are often seen thriving on the tops of banks.

Crataegus monogyna
(M–L, SU, D, ACAL, DE)

Crataegus monogyna is renowned for its profuse flow-ering in May. It is smothered in red berries in the autumn and has spiky branches, so it needs to be han-dled with care. This deciduous plant is a classic in the countryside around farmers' fields and, as it attracts

Crataegus monogyna.

nature, should be left unpruned until the end of January. The birds will feed extensively on it during the winter, if it is left alone.

Hawthorns may be found in bare-root form in suppliers' mixed hedging sections in the winter months, often advertised as 'quicks'. Nurseries offer whips in 20-cm (8-in) increments, starting from 40–60cm, then 60–80cm, and so on. They are also available in pots, but this is an expensive way of creating a hawthorn hedge.

If there are gaps in an existing hawthorn hedge, it is not wise to try to fill them in with more plants of the rose family. Instead, it will be more effective to use something unrelated, such as holly.

Cupressus

See 'Conifers'.

Cytisus Battendieri

See 'Wall Shrubs'.

Elaeagnus

Elaeagnus, in the family of Elaeagnaceae, offers valu-able, lush-foliaged evergreens for a dense natural divide. They may be used as stand-alone plants in the garden, with good ornamental properties, and also within a hedge. There are three main types (along with many forms that are less well known): the *ebbingei* types, which generally prefer a sunny position and are evergreen; the *pungens* types, which are shade-tolerant and also evergreen; and the *angustifolia* types, which are deciduous and sun-loving. They all thrive on poor soils – even on an old building site – and hate waterlogged ground. It is perfectly normal for the new growth to be brown to begin with. After ten years or more, the plants may lose the odd branch or section, but not always. If these are pruned out, they can take a while to fill back in. Another possible issue is coral spot, which appears as orange spots – any affected material definitely needs to be removed.

Elaeagnus × ebbingei
M–L, SU, D, ACAL, EV

This is a bushy evergreen that is capable of 2.5–3m (8–10ft) and gets there pretty quickly. It thrives on

Elaeagnus ebbingei.

impoverished soils and gives some fragrant late summer flowers, into early autumn, and red, peardrop-shaped fruits. The underside of the leaf is a refreshing contrast of silver to the green upper side. This variety will create a bushy divide relatively quickly. The best, bushiest ones are usually found within fifteen miles or so from the sea.

Elaeagnus ebbingei 'Limelight'
M, SU, D, ACAL, EV

Slightly less vigorous than its parents, this variety is very striking with its suffused gold foliage splash in the middle of the leaf and a green margin around the outside. It is a good plant for exposure. It loves living near the sea and will make a lovely seven-foot divide. It is not massively tough inland, however, where the winter

Elaeagnus ebbingei 'Limelight'.

temperature can stay below freezing, even in the daytime. It definitely performs better in a sunny position, but is not good for locations where it is not possible to achieve a really free-drained planting. As with all variegated plants, it is important to make sure that is checked regularly for any green parts; these should be removed, so that the plant does not revert to plain green.

Elaeagnus pungens 'Maculata'
M, SUSH, D, ACAL, EV

This is a fairly slow form compared with the *ebbingei* types, attaining six feet in height and spread. It grows best in light shade. It has a wider habit than the *ebbingei* types, which are more upright, and therefore takes more clipping if it is to be kept as a narrow divide. Again, any green leaves should be removed if they have been green for a while and do not appear to be changing to the variegation as they should – a suffused golden splash of colour in the middle of the leaf. It is a tough evergreen for windy sites, and definitely more

Elaeagnus pungens 'Maculata'.

Elaeagnus pungens 'Coastal Gold'.

All varieties thrive on poor, free-draining soil and therefore do very well on a mound or bund. They will really struggle inland during the winter months, especially if there are long periods of sub-zero temperatures. The further inland it is, the sparser the plant will be through the winter. The odd black spot can be found on the foliage, usually after wetter weather.

Escallonia is in the Grossulariaceae family, related to flowering and edible currants also known as Ribes. There are many ornamental forms; the two described below are particularly suitable to grow as a living divide in a coastal garden.

Escallonia 'Iveyi'
M, SU and semi SH, D, ACAL, semi EV

'Iveyi' is a lovely white-flowered form that is semi-evergreen. If clipped regularly on the sides, it should reach 1.5–1.8m (5–6ft) in ten years. It is probably the most reliably evergreen of the many varieties of Escallonia that are commonly used in hedging.

reliable closer to the seaside. Its leaves seem more leathery and slightly more pointy than those of its counterparts.

Elaeagnus pungens 'Coastal Gold'
M, SUSH, D, ACAL, EV

The foliage of 'Coastal Gold' is more elliptical than that of 'Maculata' and it is more upright in habit than most of the other pungens varieties. It is capable of 2.5m (8ft) in height, if clipped regularly. If it is grown up through the branches of a tree, where it will be regularly supported, it may grow much taller than this, perhaps up to 4.5m (15ft) tall. It is very striking in shade.

Escallonia

This is a must for gardeners who live near the sea, flowering profusely in the summer with a range of colours, from whites and pinks through to almost reds.

Escallonia iveyi.

Escallonia 'Apple Blossom'.

Euonymus europaea.

Escallonia 'Apple Blossom'
M, SU and semi SH, D, ACAL, semi EV

'Apple Blossom' has a naturally more upright habit, so it is easier to achieve a six-foot hedge with it. The flowers are pink. All varieties flower better when they are given a sunny situation.

Euonymus (Spindleberry)

There is a diverse range of *Euonymus* shrubs, both evergreen and deciduous. Many of the ornamental ones are used in stand-alone situations in gardens, providing interest at different times of the year, depending on the varieties. They are related to a plant called *Celastrus* and they are in the family of Celastraceae, which thrives in very dry conditions. All euonymus plants are listed as poisonous to humans, although they are not toxic to wildlife. Generally, they are very easy to look after, although they are sometimes susceptible to mildews, usually when they are in a sheltered, almost windless situation. All Euonymus can also suffer from vine-weevil attack to their roots. They prefer well-drained soils.

Euonymus europaeus
L, semi SH and heavy SH, D, ACAL, DE

The *europaeus* varieties are often sold in the winter in bare-root form for hedging. They are also available in containers in the growing season, but this is of course a more expensive option. This form loses its leaves, which have a fiery red autumn colour, followed by orange and purple calices in the winter. It is capable of reaching a height of 3.5–4.5m (12–15ft). A very good wildlife plant, it is a must for a mixed living divide of about 2.5m (8ft). It is quite upright in habit so it will not take up much space, while at the same time offering a good height.

Euonymus fortunei Varieties
S, SUSH, D, ACAL, EV

The *fortunei* types are evergreens that thrive in dry shade. If they are going to be planted in a really

Euonymus fortunei 'Emerald and Gold'.

Euonymus fortunei 'Silver Queen'.

Euonymus fortunei 'Emerald Gaiety'.

Euonymus fortunei 'Sunspot'.

inhospitable position, such as under a huge conifer, they will need to be given a healthy start, with some soil-based compost and watering to get them established. There are a number of varieties to look out for: *Euonymus fortunei* 'Sunspot', though a little prone to reversion, has a suffused yellow splash in the centre of its leaf, with a green margin, allowing it to be better in windy situations; *Euonymus fortunei* 'Emerald and Gold' is the other way round in its colouring, with gold on the outside of the leaf and green on the middle; *Euonymus fortunei* 'Emerald Gaiety' has silver sides to the leaf and a green middle, as does *Euonymus fortunei* 'Silver Queen', which has a wider, more striking edge of silver and a slightly bigger leaf that is still green in the middle. All the varieties will change colour in cold exposure, generally producing heavy tinges of pink. 'Silver Queen' can be planted with its back against an inert support, such as a fence, trellis or wall, where it can reach six feet plus, if left long enough.

All these varieties should be spaced 40cm (15in) apart. Planted alongside a semi-shaded pathway, they will grow into a colourful two-foot edge that will need pruning only once a year. They will be very happy on free-draining soil.

Euonymus japonicus Varieties
S–M, SU, D, ACAL, EV

The *japonicus* types prefer a well-drained soil and a sunny location, especially if they are variegated. The

Euonymus japonicus 'Ovatus Aureus'.

green ones are slightly more shade-tolerant. As with all variegated plants, it is important to remove any persistent green sections, to prevent reversion. Generally, these are more upright in habit, so they can be kept as a small living divide – four feet high is quite achievable. There are many that are used as stand-alone forms within the garden. A couple that grow well as a hedge are *Euonymus japonicus*, which is plain green, and *Euonymus japonicus* 'Ovatus Aureus', which has golden margins to green in the middle of the leaves. These are more likely to get mildews in the shade, especially if they are very protected from wind, for example, under a tree canopy.

Garrya

See 'Wall Shrubs'.

Griselinia Littoralis
M–L, SU and light SH, D, ACAL, EV

Also known as New Zealand broadleaf, this plant provides probably one of the most refreshing lime-green-colours available. As its name 'littoralis' suggests, it particularly enjoys being near the sea – the best examples seem to all be within ten miles or so of the coast. It thrives on well-drained, poor soils, is not fussy about pH, and is very versatile. It will reach 4.5–6m (15–20ft) as an evergreen tree over a long period of time, and can be clipped into a really nice hedge of any height from about 1.5 to 3m (5 to 10ft), and kept very narrow, if pruned regularly. If it is left to its own devices or allowed to get any taller than 3m (10ft), it will definitely have less dense foliage lower down. The density will be better when the plant is kept shorter and growing in a sunny situation. The heavier the shade, the more sparse it becomes. It comes from New Zealand and is related to spotted laurel *Aucuba* and the dog-woods/pagoda woods (*Cornus*), among others. The family is known as Cornaceae.

Griselinia has insignificant greenish flowers and bluey-black fruit in the autumn, on older wood.

Hebe, Veronica
S–M, SU, D, ACAL, EV

Many hebes and veronicas come from New Zealand or Australia, and some are from South America, indicating that they are not fantastically hardy in colder climates.

Griselinia littoralis.

Hebe variety.

Griselinia littoralis in berry.

In the UK, the best examples will always be seen in coastal areas, generally less than ten miles inland for the less hardy forms. As a general rule of thumb, the smaller the leaf, the hardier it is, and the bigger the leaf, the more tender. They hold their leaves in winter. Many are grown as ornamental varieties and are really not suitable for a hedge. Where they have been grown over the years as hedges rather than as individual plants, gardeners have always been more successful with the smaller-leafed forms. These can make a nice low living divide, or 'edge hedge', around a protected sunny pathway. The taller ones often suffer in the UK winter, resulting in spring die-back each year. Hebes can be protected in a cold winter with fleece, but this is not practical where they have been grown as a hedge. All varieties require a sunny location and hate heavy soils. A freely drained soil is best.

Hebe is in the family of Scrophulariaceae, related to foxgloves and many others. The hardiest form for the UK is *Hebe rakiensis*, which has been grown for a long time. It has small, refreshing green leaves and white flowers in the summer, and makes a three-foot dome if left. It does need side pruning in order to be kept narrow as a hedge. Most varieties can be cut back hard to regenerate growth, but they should not be pruned in autumn or winter.

Hypericum 'Hidcote'
M, SUSH, D, ACAL, EV

Hypericum is sometimes planted in a municipal situation where space is not an issue. When it is in its natural form, in other words, unclipped, it will be 1.5m (5ft)

Hypericum patulum 'Hidcote'.

wide and 1.5m (5ft) high. Its branches have an arching habit. It can be clipped and kept narrow, but it will have less foliage on it during the winter if it is trained this way. It produces yellow flowers during the summer and early autumn. It is in the Guttiferae family, which is not related to most garden shrubs. There are many different types of hypericum.

Ilex (Holly)
M−L, semi SH and heavy SH, D, ACAL, mostly EV

The wonderful world of holly offers so much variety, interest and seasonality, the plant is surely on every gardener's list of favourites. Some are evergreen, some are deciduous, some have spiky leaves, some have smooth leaves, some have variegated leaves in gold or silver or white with the green, some have almost blue leaves, some are plain green, some are golden-leaved, some are silver-leaved, some have red berries, some have yellow berries, some have white berries, some have orange berries, some have black berries. In terms of growth habit, some varieties are

fastigiate or upright, some are almost prostrate, some are rounded, some are narrow, some are weeping, some are pyramidal. There are literally hundreds of varieties, many of which are eminently suitable for creating a boundary, but it is always worth planting at least one or two within any garden. Most hollies are slow-growing, but they are very permanent once they are grown. They are generally long-lived and excellent for wildlife.

Most gardeners who grow a holly hedge and keep it clipped will never see the true natural shape of this plant. There are living specimens of hollies that have not been touched by anybody, with only dead branches having been removed, at various arboretums in the UK and in other countries. Van Dusen Gardens in Vancouver is one place that has some wonderful specimens of holly growing into their natural shape, many over a hundred years old. Some have become quite domed at the top and have long, weeping outer branches. Due to its longevity, holly can be very forgiving if you have to prune it harder than normal.

Generally, if you are wanting lots of berries on various female forms, you need to plant them with male varieties nearby. There are some self-fertile varieties, but they never seem to produce as many berries as those that are planted with other male forms, to help maximize pollination. Well-drained soil is essential. They are in a family almost on their own called Aquifoliaceae. Sometimes you will see holly leaf miner damage to leaves, but, due to their longevity, they generally shake most attacks off.

Ilex aquifolium
M−L, semi SH and heavy SH, D, ACAL, EV

The lanes and small streets of most villages in the UK are adorned by holly hedges, usually adjacent to older properties, often shaped or sculptured. It is a long-lived and versatile plant that gives great results in shaded or semi-shaded boundary situations. Due to it being slow to establish, it is often used for internal divides. Plants of this variety need to be planted 40−45cm (15−18in) apart, slightly staggered, not in a straight line. This form is not specific on male and female and that is why, on more mature hedges of this type, berrying can be sporadic. Many small garden birds nest in this hedge system because it is prickly and

Ilex aquifolium.

therefore very safe from an attack from other creatures and bigger birds.

Holly enjoys conditions similar to those of a woodland floor. This is well illustrated in the New Forest, for example, where hollies grow beautifully among and beneath the larger deciduous trees. Because of this, when planting holly it is advisable to incorporate plenty of well-rotted leaves and broken-down plant material, which it would naturally be getting if it was living in a woodland environment.

Ilex aquifolium 'Silver Queen'.

Ilex Aquifolium 'Silver Queen'
M−L, semi SH and heavy SH, D, ACAL, EV

This holly is an evergreen male variety with lovely, almost white margins to its otherwise green spiky leaves. It has small white flowers in the spring and is an excellent pollinator for female forms, but it is not a berrying form. If left alone, it will reach about 4.5m (15ft). When growing it for a hedge, the plants should be spaced at roughly 45cm (18in) apart at the planting stage. This one really illuminates a shady spot and is good when kept to six to nine feet tall. It is easy to keep this variety narrow and it will probably only need to be pruned once a year.

Ilex × altaclariensis 'Golden King'
M−L, semi SH and heavy SH, D, ACAL, EV

This is an evergreen female variety that has almost smooth, rounded foliage, a suffused golden margin to the leaves, small white flowers in the spring and masses of red berries in the autumn. It should be

Ilex × altaclariensis 'Golden King'.

Ilex crenata.

planted in the vicinity of male varieties of holly to maximize its berrying potential. This one is also capable of reaching 4.5m (15ft) in height, but it is great kept to six to nine feet tall as a hedge, and it is easy to clip the sides to train it as a narrow living divide. It is excellent for semi-shade on well-drained soil. When planting, mix in lots of well-rotted leaves that are at least a year old.

Ilex crenata
S, light SH, D, ACAL, EV

Very different in appearance from the other varieties, this one has very small leaves, somewhat similar to box. It is very compact, and makes a good four-foot hedge. It is evergreen, with small white flowers in the spring and small black berries in winter. It should be planted at a maximum of 45cm (15in) spacing. It prefers slightly filtered light and well-drained soil.

There are many crenate hollies, all offering very different features, which will add to the interest when planting stand-alone varieties in a garden. This one can be used as an alternative to box, to achieve a box-like finish in semi-shade.

Juniperus

See 'Conifers'.

Lavandula Angustifolia (English Lavender)
S, SU, D, ACAL, DE

When growing lavender in the UK, it is safer to stick to *Lavandula angustifolia*, also known as English lavender, as the plants are much hardier. There are many different varieties, with lighter and darker shades of blue/ mauve, pink and white. Wet winters in the UK can cause lavender to struggle, especially on heavy soils – it thrives on freely drained stony soils. Lavender is often prone to becoming very woody, especially if it has been pruned hard in the autumn. Ideally, the plants should only be deadheaded up to the autumn, taking the flower stalk but not the foliage, and then a couple of inches of foliage can be trimmed off in the middle of February.

Lavender is often used alongside a sunny pathway and, depending on the chosen variety, stays at football size or can go up to 90cm (3ft). The same treatment is required irrespective of its size in the long term. The smaller the variety, the closer they should be planted

Lavandula angustifolia.

together – 25–30cm (10–12in) for the small ones and 35–45cm (15–18in) for the bigger ones.

Lavender is in the family Labiatae, related to *Monarda* (bergamot) and *Thymus* (thyme), among many others.

Ligustrum (Privet)

Most gardens will have some representation of privet somewhere. There are some varieties that hold their leaves and some that lose them during the winter. Most varieties berry well in the autumn, after displaying white flowers in the spring. Privet varieties are good for wildlife. An ornamental example will usually be covered in bees and hoverflies in the flowering season and have small birds tucking into the bluey-black fruits in the winter. *Ligustrum* is in the family Oleaceae, related to *Syringa* (lilac), among others. Privet is generally trouble-free, although occasionally there may be some blotchiness in the foliage, which can be viral.

Ligustrum Japonicum
M, SU, D, ACAL, EV

With a leaf almost the size, texture and colour of that of a camellia, and a bushy but upright habit, this makes an excellent evergreen hedge around six feet in height. In order to achieve success with this type in the UK, the garden needs to be relatively sheltered and not too far inland, so that the temperature does not drop below zero for too long a period of time. For really sheltered gardens, there are variegated versions too, such as *Ligustrum japonicum* 'Excelsa Superbum'. It will not enjoy a heavily shaded situation and will prefer a well-drained soil, especially when young. Due to the waxy leaves, it is slower to establish than ordinary privet. It should be started off as container-grown plants.

Generally, in the UK, the further inland you go, the more gardeners have success with semi-evergreen varieties, which will be fully deciduous in really cold areas.

Ligustrum Ovalifolium (Californian Privet)
M, SU and light SH, D, ACAL, EV to DE

In milder areas, and milder winters, this plant can hold most of its leaves through the winter, but in really cold

Ligustrum japonicum in berry.

Ligustrum ovalifolium 'Aureum' (gold).

Green *Ligustrum ovalifolium.*

Variegated *Ligustrum ovalifolium.*

Ligustrum ovalifolium – green and gold together.

and so on. This makes it cheaper to buy at that time of the year. It is much faster to establish than *L. Japonicum*, as it does not develop such thickly waxed foliage. The foliage is more rounded than that of the common privet. It still produces white flowers and black fruits and is fairly upright in habit and therefore can make quite a nice hedge to 8 feet tall and only a couple feet wide, if it is clipped regularly. It can be used in the fedge technique and also lends itself to being planted slightly staggered, as opposed to in a dead straight line, at approximately 40–45cm (15–18in) between centres. There are variegated and golden forms, none of which have quite the same vigour, so should be expected to do less in terms of dimensions. They should be planted 30–40cm (12–15in) apart.

Ligustrum Vulgare (Common Privet)
M, SU and light SH, D, ACAL, EV to DE

The common privet has narrower, more elongated foliage than the Californian privet. It has white flowers

weather it may lose them all. Because it can withstand losing its foliage, it is often sold as bare-root whips in the winter, starting at 40–60cm (16–24in) and increasing in 20-cm (8-in) increments, to 60–80cm (24–32in),

Ligustrum vulgare.

Lonicera nitida.

and black fruits and a similar upright habit. It is available either as bare-root whips in the winter, offered in 20-cm (8-in) increments, starting from 40–60cm, then 60–80cm, and so on, or in containers out of the dormant season. Like the Californian privet, it holds most of its leaves through the winter in milder areas.

Lonicera

Lonicera Nitida
M, SU and semi SH, D, ACAL, EV

This shrub honeysuckle is a very small-leaved evergreen capable of 1.5m (5ft) high. However, the taller it grows as a hedge, the more it wants to lean, as it is not overly stout, especially if it is also kept narrow. It does well therefore as a fedge, where it will enjoy the additional support. It grows together very tightly and is great for semi-shade. *Lonicera nitida* 'Baggesen's Gold' is a gold version that is more compact in height – at 90–120cm (3–4ft), it will stay in shape and not start to lean. It has occasional small creamy white flowers in spring and dark, bluey-purple fruits in the autumn. The

Lonicera nitida 'Baggesen's Gold'.

Lonicera pileata.

golden colour fades in heavy shade. It is perfectly happy on both acidic and alkaline soils.

As a shrub honeysuckle, it is in the Caprifoliaceae family and is related to *Weigela* and *Viburnum*, among others. There are many ornamental forms of honeysuckle that will stand alone and do not need support.

Lonicera pileata
S, SUSH, D, ACAL, EV

An evergreen low-growing, small-leafed shrub, which is broader than it is high, loves sun or shade and is happy in any soil, however impoverished. It is not good in waterlogged soils. If it is clipped, it can be kept quite happily at a couple of feet high. It does need trimming regularly on the sides if it is to be kept narrow. As it is almost indestructible, it is often used in municipal areas around pathways and car parks.

Osmanthus

Osmanthus are valuable evergreens that have fragrant small white flowers during late spring and black fruits in the winter. There are many ornamental forms, some of which have smooth leaves and some that are spiky-leaved. The two varieties below are particularly useful for creating a living divide. Both will live in sun or shade, which makes them very versatile. The one thing *Osmanthus* will not tolerate is heavy, wet ground, so all varieties lend themselves well to being planted on a bund. They rarely suffer from any form of disease and only look poor when the soil conditions are not right – usually when it is too wet. They are in the Oleaceae family, related to the olive and privet, among others.

Osmanthus × *Burkwoodii*
M, SUSH, D, ACAL, EV

This upright form is evergreen and capable of 1.8–2.5m (6–8ft), given time. It has fragrant white flowers in late spring and black fruits in the autumn, and is happy in sun or shade, as long as there is good drainage. It may well appear to stand still for the first 18 months, while it is establishing roots below ground. Plant at 45-cm (18-in) intervals.

Osmanthus × *burkwoodii.*

Osmanthus delavayi.

Osmanthus Delavayi
S–M, SUSH, D, ACAL, EV

A somewhat slower form of *Osmanthus*, more sprawling in habit and wider too, if left to grow alone. However, with clipping, it will perform nicely and could be capable of 1.5m (5ft), given time, but without exceeding 60cm (2ft) in width. It is very slow when first planted and often only supplied in 2-litre pots, because it is so reluctant to get going. Once established, however, it is actually quite quick. It is critical for it not to be waterlogged at its roots while it is young. The bunding method is excellent for this form, raising it up from ground level by the height of the bund from day one. It can be planted about 40cm (15in) apart.

Photinia × Fraseri 'Red Robin'
M, SU, D, AC, EV

This valuable evergreen offers fantastic contrast, with its red new growth against its bold green foliage. Full sun is best. Gardeners who have trimmed photinia

Photinia × fraseri 'Red Robin'.

outside of the summer months in the UK have suffered the consequences of a sparser appearance to the plant in future years. A trim at the end of March and then again at the end of the growing months – mid to end of June – is less risky. It must be left alone at the end of summer into autumn in the UK, otherwise it will never be the same again, because of the occurrence of wet and cold together during the winter. Good drainage is essential for this plant – it will not tolerate waterlogging – and it is unlikely to stay thick and bushy in the long run above 2.5m (8ft) in the UK. There are many ornamental versions of photinia that feature in gardens, grown as stand-alone plants. It really dislikes being planted in shallow chalky soils and will achieve much better, stronger growth on neutral to acidic soils. The foliage will look its best in an acidic situation.

Photinia is related to the rose, meaning it is in the Rosaceae family, so it needs to be planted well away from any established plants that are also related to the rose.

Pieris Japonica Forrestii 'Forest Flame'
M, SH, D, AC, EV

There are many *Pieris japonica* varieties, which come from Japan. Some are more vigorous than others, all are evergreen and some are variegated. One thing they all have in common is lots of trusses of white flowers in the spring and they often have contrasting new growth, usually pinks and reds, in the spring. The foliage is glossy, green, evergreen and lanceolated. Behind each

Pieris forestii 'Forest Flame'.

flower in the spring develops a small seed case in the autumn, along the truss, where the flowers were. *Pieris* needs well-drained, humus-rich, acidic soil. Giving it lots of well-rotted leaves and twigs when planting helps to re-create the woodland conditions that it would enjoy in its natural environment. In the UK, it is not good when it faces east, as it needs to be in a place where the early-morning sun cannot reach it; usually, facing west is best. Too often over the years *Pieris* varieties have been planted in sunny, open locations, and have been damaged by the early-morning sun in springtime. This can make the foliage look washed out, particularly in hotter parts of the UK. For this reason, it is often grown under trees. Location is particularly important when it being used to create a boundary. When it is grown as a stand-alone shrub, it can be protected with fleece during the worst of the weather, but in a boundary it will need to be able to thrive without help. In the right position, it should suffer very little.

Pieris japonica Forrestii is thick and bushy if it is trimmed annually. If it is pruned after flowering, it is often possible to achieve a second flush of foliage

contrast. Do not prune in autumn or winter. Space at 45cm (18in) to 60cm (2ft) when planting.

Pieris is related to *Rhododendron*, which is in the Ericaceae family.

Pittosporum

Pittosporum is a big family of evergreen shrubs and trees, generally with fragrant flowers. Many are native to warmer climes such as South Africa and Australasia, so in the UK they definitely grow best nearer the sea. Poor soil with good drainage is essential for them to thrive. There are many ornamental forms; the best, toughest ones are *Pittosporum tenuifolium* varieties, of which there are good numbers, in a range of sizes and leaf colours, from silvers, golds and greens to variegated and burgundies. Pittosporums are great as stand-alone plants in the right spot, and the branches are often used in flower arranging. The flowers are small, fragrant and dark purple and the fruits are small, rounded woody pods. It is related to various climbing plants such as *Sollya*, in the Pittosporaceae family. It is generally trouble-free when it has been planted in the right conditions, requiring only one annual prune, in June.

Pittosporum Tenuifolium
M–L, SU, D, ACAL, EV

This upright form has mid shiny green leaves. It is capable of 4.5–5.5m (15–18ft) if left alone and makes a lovely 1.8–2.75m (6–9ft) hedge. The plants should be spaced 45cm (18in) apart. It is excellent for bund use.

Pittosporum Tenuifolium 'Purpureum'
M, SU, D, ACAL, EV

This one is a purple version with an upright habit, slightly less vigorous than the others, but still capable of growing into a good 1.8-m (6-ft) plus hedge. It will be slightly sparser if it is not clipped. When planting, 45cm (18in) spacing is about right.

Pittosporum Tenuifolium 'Silver Queen'
M, SU, D, ACAL, EV

'Silver Queen' has a bushy habit and can be a wider plant if left alone. For those who have a sheltered garden near the sea, it will grow into probably one of

Pittosporum tenuifolium.

Pittosporum tenuifolium 'Silver Queen'.

the nicest possible 1.8–2.5m (6 to 8ft) living divides. Its foliage is variegated, giving a silvery appearance from a distance. The variation is on the outside of the leaf, so it needs shelter from cold winds. Planting 45cm (18in) apart is fine for this form. When it gets cold the foliage can take on a pinkish appearance, which will stay on for the rest of the winter.

Pittosporum Tenuifolium 'Tom Thumb'
S, SU, D, ACAL, EV

'Tom Thumb' is in complete contrast to the other varieties described here, as it is very compact in habit – really capable of only 90 to 120cm or (3 to 4ft) if left alone. Because of this, it is often used as an edging plant to a pathway in a sunny situation, with good drainage. The new growth is green and therefore contrasts well with the burgundy foliage. When the winter gets cold, the foliage gets darker.

Prunus

The *Prunus* family is a massive one, with a huge range of plants, from small shrubs through to trees. They are

Pittosporum tenuifolium 'Purpureum'.

Pittosporum tenuifolium 'Tom Thumb'.

frequently used in parks and gardens, both commercial and domestic. They all require good drainage and to be planted into clean ground – as they are all related to the rose, they need to be located well away from other established members of the same family. In terms of illness and diseases, they are susceptible to more or less all the same issues as roses.

Prunus Avium (Wild Bird Cherry)
M–L, SU, D, ACAL, DE

Usually found in nurseries in the winter, offered as field-grown bare-root whips starting at 40–60cm (16–24in) in height and increasing in 20-cm (8-in) increments. They are often with the mixed hedging.

Prunus Cerasifera, Myrobalan (Wild Plum)
M–L, SU, D ACAL, DE

This is more likely to be found as bare-root plants in the winter, often with the mixed hedging. Its fruit is often used in recipes, such as hedgerow jelly. Good drainage is essential.

Prunus Laurocerasus (Cherry Laurel)
M–L, SU and light SH, D, ACAL, EV

Next to privet, this is probably the most widely used evergreen shrub in the UK for hedging. The form *Prunus laurocerasus* 'Rotundifolia' is the one that is usually sold by suppliers. Its leaves are more rounded and less elongated than other varieties, as the name

Prunus avium.

Prunus cerasifera.

Prunus laurocerasus with its fruit.

Prunus laurocerasus 'Rotundifolia'.

go away for a while, before returning to the same truss to feed again as soon as more of the berries have turned red. In the past, laurel would have been pruned by hand with secateurs, to avoid cutting the leaves in half, which was of course very time-consuming. Nowadays, most gardeners use a powerful hedge trimmer. The root systems on this plant are very powerful once established, and will take a significant amount of nutrients from the surrounding ground.

Prunus Luscitanica (Portuguese Laurel)

M–L, SU to light SH, D, ACAL, EV

The Portuguese laurel has a smaller, dark green, glossy evergreen foliage with red petioles to its leaves, white

Prunus laurocerasus with its flowers.

'Rotundifolia' would suggest. Much of the UK has this plant and yet the flowers and fruits are very rarely seen, because it has to be pruned so regularly to keep it to size. If left alone, it will produce white flowers that are almost like miniature Buddleja flowers and in the autumn it will fruit with green, black and red berries all on the same truss, and only black fruits on 'Rotundifolia'. The birds will come and harvest the red berries, then

Prunus luscitanica.

Prunus spinosa.

flowers in the spring and purple-black fruits in the winter. It becomes a small evergreen tree if left alone and can be kept at a nice height of 1.8–3m (6–10ft), if trained as a hedge. When planting from 3-litre pots, it should be spaced at 45–60cm (18–24in).

Prunus Spinosa (Sloe)
M–L, SU, D, ACAL, DE

As its name would indicate, this is a spiky plant. It is a deciduous shrub that will reach 3.5m (12ft) plus, with clusters of white flowers in the spring and dark blue-black sloe fruits in the winter. It is usually sold in mixed hedging during the winter months as field-grown or bare-root whips, in 20-cm (8-in) increments, usually starting at 40–60 cm (16–24in). It definitely increases its level of fruit when several are planted near each other, so it is worth putting a few in together when looking to create a mixed hedge. It is important to remember when planting a mixed hedge that the chances are quite a few of the plants in the mix will be related to the rose. This means ensuring that the ground is nice and clear and does not contain any existing Rosaceae plants, or any remnants of previous plants of the same family. The fruits of the sloe are often used in recipes.

Pyracantha

See 'Wall Shrubs'.

Rhamnus Alaternus 'Argenteovariegata'

See 'Wall Shrubs'.

Rhododendron
S, M and L, Light and heavy SH, D, AC, EV

There are literally thousands of varieties of rhododen-dron, ranging from very small shrubs through to small garden trees, which develop if the shrub is left alone. They are related to *Pieris*, among many others in the Ericaceae family. The common, vigorous purple-flowering form that is considered invasive in certain

Rhododendron.

parts of the world is *Rhododendron ponticum*. There are more ornamental varieties, which, when planted in a line in a single variety, will create a living hedge within the capabilities of each particular form. Although there are variegated varieties available, potential reversion means that it is easier when planting for a living divide to use the green-leaved forms. There are literally thousands of these.

Sometimes, when rhododendrons are grown as a narrow hedge, the result will end up being quite sparse with age. Because of this, it needs an extra couple of feet to be able to grow into at its base, especially with the larger-leaved varieties. Generally, the larger-leafed rhododendrons grow into bigger plants than the smaller-leafed varieties. They do not like early-morning sun and must have an acidic soil that is humus-rich and friable. Many rhododendrons thrive the best under the canopy of bigger trees. Sometimes, the buds will survive almost to opening time and then just fall off. This is usually due to the plant having dried out too much the previous autumn. This is their thirstiest time, as they are setting bud, ready to flower the following spring.

Rosa (Rose)
S–M, SU, moist not wet, ACAL, DE

This is a huge family of plants, with some amazing shrubs, from small ones of around 60cm (2ft) and others that are capable of reaching 1.5–1.8m (5–6ft). They flower pretty well all summer long and then produce hips in the autumn and winter. These are great for the birds and used in lots of hedgerow jelly

Hedging variety of *Rosa*, with fruit.

recipes. Rose shrubs should be planted in a sunny location when young, but they will mature nicely in a mixed-hedge situation, even though many of the branches will become shaded over time. During the winter, many nurseries will offer a selection of rose varieties in the bare-root section, for hedging. They are usually sold as whips in 20-cm (8-in) increments, starting at 40–60cm (16–24in). There are also masses of different, traditional shrub roses in containers available all year round. As they are in the Rosaceae family, they need good, clean ground, well away from any other roseaceous plants that are already established, such as an old orchard tree. All roses are susceptible to the usual black spot, mildew and rust, and to aphid attack. Roses are hungry for nutrients, so lots of good soil and composts are required when planting.

Rosmarinus Officianalis (Rosemary)
S, SU, D, ACAL, EV

Whilst there are many other varieties of rosemary, growing in all sorts of ways, from prostrate, carpeting forms,

Hedging variety of *Rosa*, in flower.

Rosmarinus officianalis.

Salix (bush willows).

which are often used to soften the top of a sunny wall, to those with an upright habit, which develop into natural columns, *R. officianalis* is traditionally bushy and evergreen, with blue flowers in the summer. It always looks fabulous, as long as it is maintained and positioned correctly. Rosemary requires very free-draining ground – making it great on the top of a bund – and as much sun as it can get. Generally speaking, in the UK 'full sun' actually means midday through to 3pm during the day. The early-morning or late-afternoon sun is cooler and will not generate such a good result on plants such as rosemary and lavender. Rosemary is in the Labiatae family and is related to many other herbs, including oregano.

Salix (Willow)
M–L, SU and light SH, W, ACAL, DE

There are many different willows, from huge trees to prostrate, carpeting forms. The bush or shrub willows are the most suitable for the purpose of creating living boundaries. They come in a huge range of winter stem and bud colours, when they have lost all their leaves. All of them really enjoy exposed, wet conditions. Generally, they are suited to grow around larger spaces, such as fields surrounded by ditches. Willows love damp conditions, so in drier situations they will send out extra root systems to find the moisture. Many nurseries in the UK sell a range of bare-root whips in

the winter, usually available in 20-cm (8-in) increments, starting from 60–80cm (24–32in). They need plenty of water right around where they are planted. They must not be planted anywhere near buildings and structures that are underground, such as pipes, cables and foundations.

Sambucus Nigra (Common Elder)
M, SU and light SH, W, ACAL, DE

This versatile plant has been around many hundreds of years and is found today in hedgerows all over the UK, providing flowers for elderflower cordial and fruit for elderberry conserves. It needs careful positioning, as it looks very full during the summer months when it is in leaf, but is very sparse in the winter. As a result, it is not ideal as a living boundary, but as an internal living divide, perhaps around a veg plot, it is excellent. It is worth planting in good numbers, to ensure that there are enough fruit and flowers to crop. Related to honeysuckle, in the Caprifoliaceae family, *Sambucus* is pretty bullet-proof as a plant, growing on both acidic and alkaline soils. If all the flowers are removed for the

Sambucus nigra.

production of cordials and other edible products, the plants that have been stripped will not be able to produce autumn berries. This is one of the reasons why it is a good idea to plant them in significant numbers, as this allows some flowers to be left on. These will later produce the fruit for cooking or preserving in the autumn and the spring. The plants are available in bare-root form in winter.

Taxus

See 'Conifers'.

Thuja

See 'Conifers'.

Viburnum
M–L, SUSH, D to moist, ACAL, EV and DE

There is a massive range of *Viburnum* species, with shrubs and small garden trees that feature in gardens across the globe. There are two or three varieties that are well worth considering for growing into a hedge.

Many viburnums enjoy filtered light rather than full sun, and good drainage is essential for them. Within the ornamental species, there are varieties for every season. They are all related to honeysuckle, among others, in the Caprifoliaceae family. They are more or less trouble-free, although some gardeners have seen an increase of thrip damage in the south of England.

Viburnum Tinus (Laurustinus)
M, SUSH, D, ACAL, EV

There are at least ten varieties of *Viburnum tinus*; all are evergreen and some are variegated. They vary in their dimensions, if left alone. The most vigorous is plain *Viburnum tinus*, which is capable of twelve feet or so if left and is therefore good for a hedge of 1.8–2.5m (6–8ft). The smaller varieties include *Viburnum tinus* 'Eve Price', which will only be half the size in the same length of time. All other forms grow somewhere in between and as long as the forms are not mixed up, most of them could be used to create a hedge. The variegated ones do need protection from high winds, especially in the winter. They all offer slightly fragrant, white flowers from November to May and purple-blue fruits in clusters that develop sporadically as the flowers finish. All varieties are slower in the pot than in open ground, but they do require some patience. Because of this, it might be a good idea to use the bund technique (*see* Chapter 2).

Viburnum tinus.

Viburnum lantana.

Viburnum Lantana (Wayfaring Tree)
M–L, light SH, D to moist, ACAL, DE

V. lantana is a deciduous form that is really only available from suppliers as a bare-root plant in the winter with the mixed hedging. It is widely found in the UK in mature hedgerows around fields. It has white flowers in the spring and red fruits in the winter.

Viburnum Opulus (Guelder Rose)
M, SUSH, D to moist, ACAL, DE

The guelder rose is a deciduous shrub, capable of 1.8–2.5m (6–8ft). It is mostly found in bare-root mixes in the winter, but it may be available in a pot during the growing season. Most suppliers sell the more ornamental form of *Viburnum opulus* 'Sterile', the

red guelder rose, which has large globular flowers and no fruit, instead of the flat flowers and red fruits of the guelder rose. This is not a plant for hedging on its own. It needs to be in amongst a mixed hedge in order to achieve a result worth having.

Conifers

Conifers come in a vast range of shapes and sizes, but many hundreds of them are either too slow or too ornate, or just not sufficiently trainable, to be suitable plants for living divides. The use of the more vigorous conifers for hedges, particularly where they have been allowed to get out of hand, discourages many gardeners from including other conifers in their garden. Many are reluctant to plant a fir or a pine tree, until they understand that there are many very slow, small varieties of these plants; indeed, some are so slow, they could be grown on a small rockery. Clearly, it is important to acquire a full understanding of the varieties that are available, and to ensure that those being considered are appropriate for the proposed purpose.

The next most important considerations are the right maintenance plan for the cultivar, and the positioning of the plants – all genetically large varieties

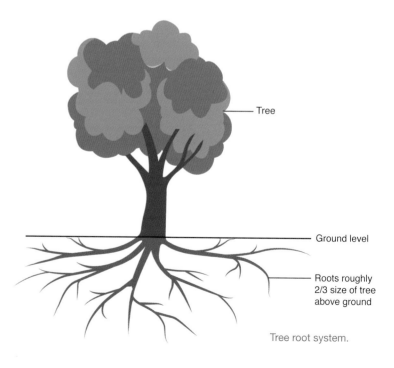

Tree

Ground level

Roots roughly 2/3 size of tree above ground

Tree root system.

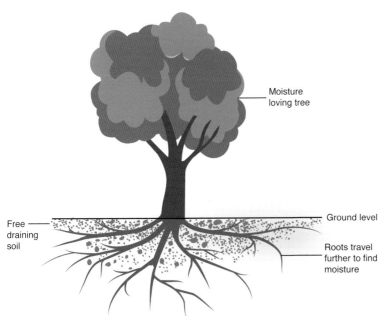

Moisture
loving tree

Ground level

Free
draining
soil

Roots travel
further to find
moisture

The root system of a moisture-loving tree.

ties will never recover. For this reason, it is very important when planting conifers for hedging to have a clear idea of its eventual size, shape and lineation. In terms of size, the most obvious issues are height and spread; the lineation refers to the training of certain sections, so that they are lower or higher than the overall hedge. If conifers are allowed to get too big, reducing them by a significant can make them look awful. If the eventual shape is planned in advance, and always kept in mind, and maintenance is regular, it will involve nothing more than taking off small amounts with a hedge cutter, as they grow. The plants will then fill up gradually, eventually creating the desired shape.

must be kept well away from buildings and any infrastructure of underground amenities and footings.

Due to the nature of many conifers, they may struggle if they have to be cut back too hard. Indeed, some varie-

Chamaecyparis Lawsoniana (Lawson's Cypress)
VL, SU, D, ACAL, EV

Although Lawson's cypress may grow very tall, there are many slower-growing, more compact varieties

Key

S	Small	Will grow less than 90cm (3ft) in ten years; easy to maintain as a low living divide. (There are hundreds of conifers in this category; small, conical forms may be planted together to create a hedge.)
M	Medium	Under 1.8m (6ft) in ten years.
L	Large	Under 3m (10ft) in ten years.
VL	Very large	All varieties that will grow faster than Large. If left unchecked, they may become too dominant in a normal domestic garden.
SU	Sunny position	
SH	Shady position	
W	Wet soils and heavy clay	
D	Dry and stony or sandy soils, and those with good drainage, or planted on mounds above heavy and wetter soils	
AC	Acidic to neutral soils	
AL	Alkaline soils	
ACAL	All soils	
EV	Evergreen	
DE	Deciduous	

A well-maintained golden variety of *Chamaecyparis lawsoniana*.

that have this plant in their parentage. Many are lovely to look at, but it is important to understand their properties, and how they need to be looked after, especially if a living divide is to be created by planting several examples of one variety. They must always be pruned within the green, gold or silver of the foliage, depending on the variety, not into the brown branch structure. If they are pruned too hard into the main structure, they will never re-shoot or colour up again. Light can only travel into a conifer a short distance, and then the foliage stops where the light stops. They therefore require regular pruning, to stop them becoming disproportionately wide. For this reason, a different option may be preferable where a narrow divide is needed, unless it is possible to incorporate twice-yearly pruning into the maintenance regime. The timing of pruning for cypress depends on geographical location: in the south of the UK, the advice is to trim once in late February, and in early March in the Midlands and in the north of the country, and then

again at the end of June. It is not a good idea to prune in the autumn or winter.

Lawson's cypress does not do well in shade; it only really thrives in a nice sunny open position, away from any structure that can cast heavy shadows close to it. Ironically, once it has established itself, and if it is allowed to get out of hand, it becomes the feature that casts everything else into the shade. It will grow in acidic and alkaline soils, as long as they are well drained while the plants are young. Once the plants are bigger, they will usually cope with slightly wetter conditions, but they will definitely struggle with waterlogging. Planting conifers in a place where others of the same family have been in the past is not a good idea. This applies especially with variants of Lawson's cypress. This cypress is related to many different conifers such as *Juniperus* (juniper) in the Cupressaceae family. Apart from conifer aphid, the usual stresses of Lawson's cypresses are long periods of drought. One problem with all the conifers is that they do not show any signs that they are too dry until it is too late to water them effectively back to health.

Cupressus (Cypress)

As with all the groups of conifers, there are many *Cupressus* varieties that are often used for more ornamental purposes. The following few are suitable for living divide situations.

Cupressus Arizonica Glauca (Silver Arizona Cypress)
M–L, SU, D, ACAL, EV

There are several *Cupressus arizonica* types grown, but for the UK the glaucous one is the best known. Originating as it does from Arizona, which has a very hot, dry climate, it is unlikely to make a good hedge inland in the UK. (The damp in the UK winter makes low temperatures seem a lot worse than they would in the drier environment of many other countries.) It will always do best in coastal areas. In the right conditions, it will have plenty of vigour and it will really need to be clipped twice a year if it is to be kept narrow. It is particularly prone to going brown if it has been cut back too hard. Good drainage and full sun are essential.

Cupressus arizonica 'Glauca' growing freely.

Cupressus macrocarpa 'Goldcrest' growing freely.

Cupressus Macrocarpa 'Goldcrest'
L-VL, SU, D, ACAL, EV

This form, one of the golden Monterey cypresses, is often found in winter display tubs alongside pansies and

An example of *Chamaecyparis Lawsoniana* (Lawson cypress) that has not been well looked after.

winter bedding plants. Released from the confines of a pot, and planted out and left alone in open soil, it will have a lot of vigour. Its colour is an asset in the garden, but it does need to be treated with care if it is to be kept as a hedge, especially near buildings. If it is left unclipped for too long, it can cause damage to nearby structures – remember, the taller the plant above ground, the bigger the root system will be below ground, to support and feed it. Cut in a tapered shape, wider at the bottom to narrower at the top, and restricted to around ten feet, it can make a really nice divide. It needs to be in full sun and have good drainage.

'Goldcrest' should be pruned in early March and at the end of June, and not in the autumn or winter. All too often, people plant it as a stand-alone feature and then neglect it, for whatever reason. Ten years later, they realize they have a huge tree in their garden. One classic error with this form is to think it needs pruning only once year, and then to go hard at it with the garden shears. This leads to the appearance of brown areas that never really recover and soon look unsightly.

× *Cupressus Leylandii* (Leyland Cypress)
VL, SU, D, ACAL, EV

This plant has become somewhat notorious as a result of garden owners buying it in large quantities and then failing to maintain it properly. It may be that they do not intend to stay in that particular house for very long, and their priority is to achieve a quick result in the time that they are living there. However, if that is the case, they would be far better advised to apply the hypotenuse technique, described in Chapter 2.

A *Leylandii* hedge can be successful, as long as its maintenance is done in text-book style – that is to say, it is possible to put in several × *Cupressus* as young plants, with a definite plan to grow them into a hedge, and keep on top of it. This means pruning it three times a year, restricting it at approximately ten feet in height, and ensuring that it is tapered in shape, narrowing at the top and broadening at its base. The tapering allows moisture to reach the outer branches all the way down the plant, particularly on the side where the wind-driven moisture would not naturally get to it. The taller the hedge and the more vertical it is, especially with conifers that are evergreen and dense, the harder it is to get moisture close to the base of the hedge, on the leeward side. This can cause branches to go brown and also make it very difficult to plant anything near the base of the hedge.

The tallest hedges in the UK usually incorporate this vigorous plant, and its presence in a garden can be a disincentive to potential house buyers, if it is within

Gold × *cupressus Leylandii* that has been allowed to grow freely.

Example of a green × *cupressus Leylandii* that has been clipped regularly.

Gold × *cupressus Leylandii* as a tall hedge.

a certain distance of buildings. Clearly, a good maintenance package is vital, but it will only be as good as the commitment to carry it out faithfully. If it slips for a year or two, the plants will probably already have started to get out of hand, and it will be too late to get them back under control. As with all *Cupressus* plants, it is important to understand that any branches that are cut beyond the last bit of foliage will never resprout. It follows that, if several branches are treated in that way, next to each other, an irretrievable bare patch will soon develop.

This is related to juniper, in the Cupressaceae family.

Juniperus (Juniper)

All shapes and sizes

There are a huge number of varieties of juniper. It is probably one of the biggest groups of ornamental conifers, and most gardens in the UK that have individual conifers will have a juniper somewhere. They are not commonly seen in use in living divides,

A silver juniper.

Gold juniper.

however, several of them in a row – perhaps *Juniperus communis*, *J. chinensis* or *J. virginiana* types – might be successful when planted together. One thing they have in common is that the juvenile growth is very sharp to the touch, even though it looks soft. Regular trimming will be essential for the more vigorous forms.

Taxus Baccata (Yew)
M–L, SUSH, D, ACAL, EV

The yew is famous in the UK. Known as the hedge with the edge, because it is so trainable, it is also the pre-ferred conifer for topiary and other detail clipping. Its close-knit growth allows the creation of really sharp edges. It is extraordinarily long-lived – some UK speci-mens are literally thousands of years old. The whole plant is poisonous, including the red fruits that appear in the winter. There are many ornamental forms, from small gold columns to carpeting forms, and all sorts in between. It is capable of living for so many years because it has many mechanisms that help it survive. If it is pruned incredibly hard, even back to the trunk, or

Taxus baccata, regularly shaped.

Thuja plicata.

has suffered from the removal of more material than necessary, it will fully recover and look really green again. It does take a while to fill back in, but it does it eventually. It may be planted to create a hedge in many different locations, on acidic and alkaline soils and in sun and shade. It is drought-tolerant but it really dislikes waterlogged soils.

It is not related to many other conifers, so it really ends up being more versatile.

Thuja Plicata (Western Red Cedar)
L–VL, SU and light SH, D, ACAL, EV

There are many ornamental forms of *Thuja*, some of which are relatively slow-growing and more compact, with many colouring up in the winter months. One in particular, *Thuja plicata* (also known as western red cedar), is a fantastic plant for quick results. It also has better tolerance of drought and shade than any others of the species, as well as rejuvenating properties. This naturally means that it can be pruned harder and it will recover, although it may take a while. It gives off a citrus fragrance when it has been pruned, adding to its appeal.

The best results with this type of hedge will be achieved by really being on top of the pruning. The aim should be to develop a tapered living divide, wider at the base and narrower at the top, allowing moisture and light to reach much more of the plant. The western red cedar is a big tree if left alone, so it should not be planted near buildings. Acidic and alkaline soils will be fine.

Needle scorch can be a problem with *Thuja*, usually caused by putting the plants in too close together,

Thuja plicata 'Zebrina'.

allowing humidity to increase between them. The best spacing is two feet apart, especially If there is a hard structure down one or both sides of the hedge, reducing the ability for the roots to spread out laterally from the line in which they are planted. If a hedge of *Thuja* is planted too close together, it is unlikely ever to perform very well, without showing some browning. It may be possible to improve an existing hedge that is too dense by taking out every other plant in the winter, and leaving it to recover. It may take a number of years, but it might end up looking fabulous.

T. plicata is related to many different conifers in the Cupressaceae family. There is also a variegated form called *T. plicata* 'Zebrina', which is slightly slower in growth, and quite happy planted at 50cm (20in) apart.

The root system of a wall shrub that has been left unsupported.

Wall Shrubs

The difference between wall shrubs and other shrubs is that the root system of the wall shrub goes down rather than out, looking for the water table. This means that it can be planted near a wall and not break into the foundations. It should always be planted just under a foot (30cm) away from the wall, leaning in towards it, rather than right up against it. There are two reasons for this. One is because of the availability of moisture – it is very dry right up against the foot of most walls. The second reason is to prevent the root system fighting the foundations as it grows downwards.

In order to support wall shrubs in the garden, fence panels and trellis systems are really good. These particular varieties tend to lean, as they lack support roots and therefore they need the extra help of being tied on to an inert support. Training involves tying in the new, developing growth in the desired direction, to create a fan shape or a column. They need a deep hole when planting, with have lots of loose soil in the bottom, to grow into from day one.

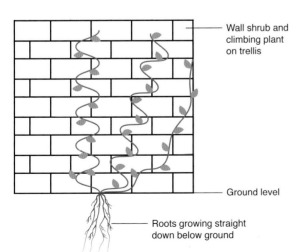

The root system of a wall shrub that is supported by trellis.

Key

S	Small	Under 1.5m (5ft) in ten years
M	Medium	Under 3m (10ft) in ten years
L	Large	Over 3m (10ft) in ten years
SU	Sunny position	
SH	Shady position	
W	Wet and heavy soils	
D	Dry and well-drained soils	
AC	Acidic to neutral soils	
AL	Alkaline soils	
ACAL	All soils	
EV	Evergreen	
DE	Deciduous	

The following few wall shrubs will be suitable for planting in groups of the same variety, to create a living divide or to soften an inert divide.

Ceanothus (California Lilac)
S–M, SU, D, ACAL, EV

Most *Ceanothus* are evergreen, but not all, and they generally have blue flowers, but there are pinks and whites too. They all love a hot sunny position with very good drainage; a gravelly soil is best. Some are more vigorous than others. If they are to grow well as a living divide in a garden that is not coastal, they will need plenty of looking after in the winter, with a protected sunny site, away from north and east winds, against a wall or fence. The emphasis is on shelter and protection. The toughest varieties are the smaller-leafed types, such as *C. impressus* 'Pugets Blue', which tend to be less upright or vigorous than the bigger-leafed varieties. They are related to *Rhamnus* (buckthorn), in the Rhamnaceae family.

Ceanothus.

Cotoneaster.

Frost damage is probably the most common problem for this species.

Cotoneaster
S-L, SUSH, D, ACAL, EV and DE

Depending on the height required for a particular spot against a wall, trellis or fence system, there are four main *Cotoneaster* varieties that are suitable: *Cotoneaster Cornubia, Cotoneaster exburiensis, Cotoneaster lacteus* and *Cotoneaster horizontalis*. For more information on these varieties, *see* Chapter 3, 'Hedging Plants'.

Cytisus Battendieri (Moroccan Broom)
M, SU, D, ACAL, semi EV

A favourite shrub, this works well when treated like a wall shrub, tied back to some trellis. It is silvery-grey, semi-evergreen, and pineapple-scented, with fragrant yellow flowers during early to midsummer. In the wild, where it comes from, it thrives in very free-draining and stony soil, so it is not very good in heavy soils, especially those that hold too much moisture or become waterlogged. In the UK, it is essential to have a sunny location, ideally from mid-morning through to the evening. The best examples are usually found not very far inland in the UK, especially if they are planted in the Midlands and the north. They are sometimes grown as a tree, but they are prone to sections becoming brittle with age. The shrubs are generally more reliable.

Cytisus battendieri.

It is related to *Robinia*, among others, in the Leguminosae family. It is absolutely beautiful for a west-facing fence that needs a plant in front of it.

Garrya (Silk Tassel Bush)
S–M, SH, D, ACAL, EV

This wonderful plant loves a position of shade with well-drained soil. Heavy wet soils are too much for it, especially when it is young and trying to establish itself. It is evergreen and the toughest ones in the UK are *Garrya elliptica* types. None of them are very good with exposure to wind, so the backing of a fence or wall is preferable. It is relatively slow to establish itself, so it is no good where a quick result is required. However, because the growing is slow, it can be easily trained to how it needs to be. There are many other shrubs and trees with tassels, but this is in its own family, Garryaceae.

Pyracantha (Firethorn)
S–M, SUSH, D, ACAL, EV

This is a familiar evergreen for sun and shade. As long as it has good drainage, and is well away from any other plants that are in the rose family, it will grow well on acidic and alkaline soils. It comes under wall shrubs because it is not very good at staying upright without any additional support, such as trellis. It is often seen leaning well away from a wall where it originally started, because the ties have not been checked and it has begun to stray. There are some small, shrubby pyracanthas, but thought needs to be given to their planting location, as they are covered in spikes that

Garrya.

Pyracantha.

could catch on a passer-by. The taller forms would generally be planted well back from a pathway. If supported – planted on either side of a piece of trellis and tied in regularly – they could be kept to around eight feet tall and only a foot or two wide. There are red-, yellow- and orange-berried forms and they all have masses of white flowers in the spring.

Pyracantha is related to the apple, along with many, many others in the Rosaceae family. It can suffer from scale insect and aphid attack, but fortunately it is low enough to treat fairly readily with sprays on calm weather days. It is fabulous for wildlife, insects and birds.

Rhamnus Alaternus 'Argenteovariegata'
M, SUSH, D, ACAL, EV

Probably one of the most under-used evergreen wall shrubs, the Italian buckthorn is seen in many different situations and does well in sunny locations as well as shady ones. It has beautiful, strong variation of silver-white margins to the leaves, which are green in the middle, white flowers in the spring and black fruits in the winter. It is thornless, though it is a buck-

thorn. It is related to *Ceanothus*, in the Rhamnaceae family.

Bamboo

A gardener's choices may have a significant effect on their neighbours as well as themselves, so it is vital to get the right information at the outset. It is so important to choose the right plant for the right situation.

Bamboo venturing through the boundary from next door.

Rhamnus alaternus 'Argenteovariegata'.

Bamboo is in a separate category here because it requires a disproportionate amount of preparation before being planted in the domestic garden, or as a living boundary. It should not be planted where its roots might interfere with drainage systems, pathways or driveways. Bamboo can certainly do this if it is given time and is unrestrained. It may be lovely to look at, but it is extremely difficult to remove, due to the distance the roots can travel over time. An established clump of bamboo may appear to be three feet or so across above the ground, while under the ground it may have spread to three times that width. It may need hours of digging and digging and digging to get all the roots out.

Cutting bamboos in half above ground also sends a message to the root system to begin spreading outwards, away from the middle. Some bamboos are described as 'clump-forming', but this will only be the case if they are not pruned and even then their spread will be 'indefinite'. Because of this, proper preparation and the use of specialist retainers are a must. This is one case where it is probably advisable to pay for the fitting and supply of professional root retainers. When planting up to an existing fence system, the root retainer will also have to be alongside the fence, otherwise the bamboo will be popping up next door to annoy the neighbours. Retainers vary massively in price, but it is worth spending enough to ensure that the quality is very strong and that they will be fit for purpose in the long term. This is the only way to achieve a successful bamboo planting.

CHAPTER 4

CLIMBING PLANTS

Climbing plants are only able to climb if they are given a support to travel up or along; really, when they have no support, they are ground-cover plants. This means that the root systems just go downwards to find moisture, and they do not need support roots. However, they do need a lot of moisture, as the base of the plant and its roots may be many feet away from the flowers or fruits that are being supported on the plant. When covering the ground, the plant will naturally want to layer itself, because this is a way for the stems to achieve further rooting and therefore take up more moisture to sustain the flowers or fruits that are further along their stems, away from the original root source.

When planting climbing plants, it is always worth preparing a very deep hole, but it does not need to be very wide. The bottom of the hole should have plenty of loose soil for the plant to grow into directly, underneath the root system, and the hole should be the same width as the pot on the plant at time of purchase. This will help the plant establish itself much faster. Climbers that are lacklustre are usually struggling below ground, due to a lack of preparation prior to planting. There is often a pan layer about 25–45cm (10–18in) below ground; if the digging breaks through that, the young climbing plant will grow much faster and perform much better as a result. Preparation is

everything, especially if the plant is going to be trained on to a support above ground, where it will never be able to layer its own root systems further along its stems, as it will no longer be in touch with the ground.

Some of the woodier-stemmed climbers will not flower for a few years or more. This is because the roots need time to take up enough moisture to sustain those flowers that grow such a long way from the plant's base.

Key

S	Small	Under 3m (10ft) in ten years
M	Medium	Between 3 and 6m (10 and 20ft) in ten years
L	Large	Above 6m (20ft) in ten years
SU	Sunny position	
SH	Shady position	
W	Wet and heavy soils	
D	Dry and well-drained soils	
AC	Acidic to neutral soils	
AL	Alkaline soils	
ACAL	All soils	
EV	Evergreen	
DE	Deciduous	

Akebia Quinata (Chocolate Vine)
L, SUSH, D, ACAL, semi EV

The chocolate vine can be very vigorous, holding fifty per cent of its leaves in the winter, and even more where it is growing in a well-protected position. It has

Akebia quinata in flower.

Akebia quinata with fruit.

fragrant purple flowers in the spring and purple banana-like fruits in the autumn. It definitely needs to be trained carefully if the aim is for it to fill up a trellis support, otherwise it will rush to the top and leave the lower parts of the support empty and still in full view. It is not suitable for growing on to living supports, as it will smother the host. It is related to several more unusual plants that are not very likely to be in the average garden, but it will not enjoy being planted close to other members of the Lardizabalaceae family.

Clematis (Virgin's Bower)
S, M and L, SUSH, W, best on AL, EV and DE

There are a number of rules relating to the growing of clematis. As long as the various guidelines are followed, they are reliable and easy plants; otherwise, they can be quite difficult. Predominantly, they love cool roots, warmer tops and a support structure near

Clematis alpina and *macropetala varieties* (pruning Group One).

Clematis viticella (pruning Group Three).

to the ground. However, there are exceptions to this rule. They prefer lime, or alkaline soils. Where the soil is acidic, providing there are no acid-loving plants already growing in the area, this can be resolved by putting a lump of chalk under the clematis when planting.

In terms of pruning and maintenance, clematis fall into three main groups when they are being grown as a living divide. (There are herbaceous forms that need less attention, as they die down to soil level each winter.) When sold, the group of a clematis plant will be specified by a number One, Two or Three on the label.

Group One incorporates varieties such as *Clematis Montana*, which are generally early-flowering and vigorous. These need to be trained as really they should be pruned only once every three years after flowering. As a result, they have two years' worth, or more, of vigorous growth to wrangle into some sort of order, whether on a piece of stand-alone trellis or against a fence. Too often, *C. montana* is planted against an inert object such as a trellis or fence and left

to its own devices. All it does is grow quickly up the fence and run along the top, leaving the whole of the rest of the fence panel or trellis bare. Training it across an inert support in an upward zig-zag fashion can be really effective. (For more on training, *see* Chapter 5.) Because they cannot be pruned every year, Group One clematis should not be grown up through or over live plant supports such as trees, shrubs or hedgerows. They will quickly smother or swamp the host.

Group Twos need to be pruned twice a year, first in the middle of February, taking 15cm (6in) off the top of each stem. It will then flower in the spring and very early summer, and need a second prune around the second week of June, just after the spring flowers are over, taking off another 15cm (6in). This will encourage it to flower again in early autumn. If it is not pruned in June, it will not produce a second flush of flowers. *Clematis* 'Nelly Moser' is probably the best-known variety in this group, but the pink bars on its flowers will fade in too much sun. *Clematis* 'Bees' Jubilee' may be a better alternative in order to achieve the Nelly Moser look in a sunny location. The base of the plant still needs to be cool, however. One trick is to position a flowerpot full of seasonal interest in front of the clematis during the growing season, to prevent the sun reaching its bottom couple of feet. Group Two comprises a huge range of colours. Like the Group Ones, they do not really lend themselves well to being grown up through live supports such as trees and shrubs – trying to find the ends to take off the requisite six inches is a difficult thing to do on a flourishing living support.

Group Three clematis have a relatively easy care package: the stems are severed at 45cm (18in) from the ground in the second week of February every year. A good trick is to leave the cane on at planting time, as a permanent marker to cut back to. If old stems from the previous year are left, the clematis will use them like a ladder to climb back up in the spring, through the shrub, tree or hedge system. The old stems will simply go brittle and fall apart during the year. Varieties in this group are brilliant for growing up through trees and shrubs, as they only have one year's growth to support. From the pruning time in February, it will grow on until midsummer, from which time it will produce flowers well into autumn. *Clematis viticella* varieties are particularly good for this job of growing up through a live support.

Note: growing any climbers through many of the conifers is a non-starter.

Group Two and Group Three clematis may be buried an extra four inches up the stem at planting time, allowing them to divide underground and throw up many more stems. This reduces the risk of clematis wilt, and also makes a much stronger plant in the long run. Clematis wilt is less likely to happen when there is plenty of structure low down to support the stems of the clematis as near to its base as possible.

Clematis are related to *Aquilegia* (granny's bonnet), among others, in the Ranunculaceae family.

Fallopia Baldschuanicum (Russian Vine)
L, SU, W, ACAL, DE

Also known as 'mile a minute' or the Russian vine, this was classified in the past as *Polygonum baldschuanicum*. It is an incredibly vigorous, deciduous, twining climber, which definitely requires training and is only suitable for growing on to inert supports. If this plant is simply put into the ground and then left alone, it quickly becomes the thug of the garden and swamps everything in its path. It will grow in anything except the most waterlogged soils and will need regular attention and tying in. If it is planted near to a fence and not trained, it will quickly and easily reach the top of the fence and then just run along the top, leaving the whole of the bottom three-quarters with nothing on it. It has white summer and autumn flowers. It is related to *Muehlenbeckia complexa* (wire vine), among others, in the Polygonaceae family.

Hedera (Ivy)
M, SH, D, ACAL, EV

Many people avoid ivy, because they have seen the damage it can do to brickwork, particularly the pointing. It can also completely take over trees, swamping them over time, and can force itself between the slats of larch lap and feathered fence systems. However, if it is used carefully it offers tremendous benefits and is amazing

Fallopia baldschuanicum.

Hedera *colchicum* variety, at the back of the border.

Hedera in arborescent state with fruit.

Hydrangea petiolaris.

for wildlife. It can be used very effectively on close-knit trellis of wood or wire mesh, is good on solid concrete, where there are no gaps, and is excellent for covering dead tree stumps or unattractive gate posts. It has roots on its stems so it is great in really dry situations. The smaller-leaved forms are the toughest, and the large-leaved forms are often very striking, especially if they are variegated. Those with variegated margins on their leaves need more protection from winter winds. They are mostly tolerant of heavy shade and drought.

After ten years or more, the plant starts to mutate. Its leaves change shape and it becomes arborescent – that is to say, it develops into a tree in its own right. This is quite something for wildlife. At this point it produces white flowers and then black fruits in profusion, through the winter months. The plant then slows down significantly, no longer creeping along trying to get the moisture from anywhere it can. It is related to *Fatsia*, among others, in the Araliaceae family. The most common maintenance issue is that it needs to be checked for reversion on variegated varieties. This means removing any plain green leaves from the plant, but not too soon, as it can take several months for the coloured parts to develop.

Hydrangea Petiolaris (Climbing Hydrangea)
M–L, SH, W, ACAL, DE

The climbing hydrangea, with its deciduous white summer-flowering lace, is vigorous when it gets going – it is capable of covering several fence panels, given time. Once established, it enjoys moist ground. It will self-grip a wall or fence with small pads like feet on its stems. It can damage soffits on buildings and it is not a good idea to plant it against rendered walls or where there is lots of mortar. It will prefer a position where it will not catch the early-morning sun if possible. It is related to *Philadelphus* (mock orange), among others, in the Hydrangeaceae family.

Jasminum (Jasmine)
Jasminum nudiflorum: M, SUSH, D, ACAL, DE
Jasminum officianale: M–L, SU, D, ACAL, DE

Probably the most effective position for jasmine is on a piece of trellis, dividing the ornamental garden from the more functional garden. A *Jasminum nudiflorum* (winter jasmine) can be positioned in sun or shade in view of the house, for some winter interest to enjoy from indoors. The summer jasmines, such as *J. officianale*, can be run all along trellising for summer fragrance, to be enjoyed while out in the garden. Jasmine that is allowed to grow up through a live support could throttle it in the long run. The summer jasmines need lots of sunlight in order to flower, and some of them are not

Jasminum nudiflorum.

reliably hardy. Good drainage is essential as jasmines hate waterlogged ground. They are in the Oleaceae family, related to *Osmanthus* as well as many others.

Lathyrus Latifolia (Perennial Sweet Pea)
S, SUSH, D, ACAL, DE

The perennial sweet pea is generally very reliable, providing lots of summer colour, although the flowers are not fragrant, unlike the annual varieties. It dies back in the winter and comes back up five or six feet every year. It seems to be fine on all sorts of ground, from very chalky to very acidic, although it does not like waterlogged soil. Available with mauve/red, white or pink flowers, it readily pods in the autumn and it is well worth collecting the seeds and sowing them to increase the number of plants. It is not fussy about either full shade or full sun, although it seems to flower more profusely in a sunnier location than in heavy shade. It may even flower successfully up into the middle of a tree, where it will receive only a limited amount of light during the growing season. Because it dies down in the winter, it grows happily with other

Jasminum officianale.

Lathyrus latifoila.

living supports. It is related to *Wisteria*, among many others, in the Leguminosae family.

Lonicera (Honeysuckle)

Lonicera periclymenum types: L, SH, humus-rich soil, ACAL, DE
Lonicera japonica types: L, SUSH, W and D, ACAL, SEMI EV

The honeysuckle family comprises both shrubs and climbing plants. (For information on shrub honeysuckles, *see* the listings in Chapter 3.) There are many varieties of climbing honeysuckle available to gardeners in the UK, offering all sorts of benefits. Due to their more permanent woody structure, they are better on inert supports than going through a live support. Suitable for shade, the *Lonicera periclymenum* types, also known as woodbine, lose their leaves in winter. Most are fragrant and they do best in woodland settings. *L. periclymenum* 'Belgica', the Dutch early honeysuckle with its pink and yellow flowers, combines very well with *L. periclymenum* 'Serotina', the Dutch late, which has red and yellow flowers. This combination will provide flowers from April into summer, from the Dutch early, and on into autumn, from the Dutch late. They

Lonicera japonica 'Halliana'.

have plenty of vigour, so they should be trained back and forth on the trellis to get the best results. There are many other *L. periclymenum* varieties to choose from. Mixing plenty of old leaves in with the soil when planting will simulate the woodland setting that they enjoy.

For sunny locations there are semi-evergreen varieties such as *L. japonica* types, which are long-flowering and vigorous, and will be happy in any soil, except a waterlogged one. *Lonicera* is related to *Viburnum*, among others, in the Caprifoliaceae family. Probably the most common issue with honeysuckle, other than mildews in the spring, is early desiccation of the foliage, when a shade-loving variety has been exposed to too much sun.

Muehlenbeckia Complexa (Wire Vine)

L, SH, D, ACAL, EV

The wire vine has plenty of vigour and is almost evergreen, especially close to the sea where the winter does not hit in the same way as it does further inland. It produces a very frothy effect, with its small-leaved foliage and small fragrant flowers in July and August. It will grow in the most arid of soils in the shade. It is best to grow it through an inert support, unless its live support

Lonicera periclymenum 'Serotina', with flowers just starting to open up.

Muehlenbeckia complexa (wire vine).

Passiflora caerulea.

is enormous, such as a bear-trunked pine tree that has forty feet before the lowest branches. It is related to rhubarb, among others, in the Polygonaceae family.

Passiflora (Passion Flower)
M−L, SU, D, ACAL, EV

There are hundreds of different passion flowers world-wide, but the variety most commonly used in the UK is *Passiflora caerulea,* known as the blue passion flower, which is definitely the toughest. Passion flowers love a really sunny location in poor soil. It is possible to grow some of the less tough varieties in the UK, but they will survive only in a particularly sheltered garden, or with some added protection in the winter, such as Perspex. It is in the Passifloraceae family, not related to much else. In a favourable situation it is capable of swamping a living support, so it is definitely better grown on a wall or other inert support.

Pileostegia Viburnoides
S−M, semi SH, D, ACAL, EV.

Also known as the climbing hydrangea, this is good grown against a shady garden wall, but it will demand

Pileostegia viburnoides.

patience, as it is slow to establish. For the first couple of years it will seem to do not very much above ground, but it will put on roughly 45cm (18in) from then on, in the growing season. It has large, leathery, evergreen foliage and wonderful white flowers in the summer. It will be fine in any soil except a waterlogged one, so it is wise to incorporate grit when planting in heavy soils. It is related to the hydrangea in the Hydrangeaceae family.

Rosa (Rose)
S - L, SU, D, ACAL, DE

There are many different varieties of climbing and rambling roses. Climbing roses produce flowers on and off through the summer months and the rambling roses will do a one-off show of flowers. Many of the rambling roses are pretty vigorous, whereas with the climbing roses, there are plenty of smaller-growing forms and some vigorous ones. There are a few evergreen climbing roses available, but they are not good with exposure and require the backing of a wall or fence in most

Pink climbing rose.

cases. The family into which the roses fall is very large and there are many plants related to them. The difficulty with this is that they really dislike being planted in a location where established members of the same family are already growing. To keep roses really healthy, it is important to plant them away from the existing root systems of any rose family member. They are also hungry, so they need plenty of enriched soils around the roots when preparing for planting.

The different climbing and rambling roses vary hugely in terms of their ability to fend off the usual array of attacks from mildews, rusts and black spots. Some varieties are definitely more resilient than others, but in certain weather conditions, most roses will be showing some signs of these ailments by midsummer, if they are not regularly sprayed. It is important to vary the sprays – using just one fungicide or one insecticide during the growing season will not be effective. Aphids and greenfly will also tend to make an appearance around the new buds and on the new growth. To avoid over-use of chemicals, which can be so harmful to the environment and to wildlife, the best advice is to choose varieties on the basis of their reliability and disease resistance, especially when using them to grow on trellis as part of a living divide. Some varieties will require much less spraying than those that are

Pink rambling rose.

Solanum.

Trachelospermum jasminoides.

more disease-prone. Interestingly, black spot is more likely to appear on roses in areas of very clean air, well away from industry and other pollutants.

Roses are related to *Spiraea*, among many others, in the Rosaceae family.

Solanum (Nightshade)
M–L, SU, D, ACAL, DE

The toughest forms of ornamental nightshades for the UK are the *Solanum jasminoides* varieties, which have blue/white-tinted flowers all summer. *S. jasminoides* 'Album' has white summer flowers. These varieties have plenty of vigour for a sunny position and do not mind a poor soil, as long as it drains well. The other classic variety for the UK is *S. crispum* 'Glasnevin', which is more of a shrubby climber and definitely not as vigorous as the *S. jasminoides* types, although it enjoys the same sort of environment as them. It has blue flowers throughout the summer.

Solanums are in the large Solanaceae family, related to tobacco, among others.

Trachelospermum
M, SU, D, AC, EV

Trachelospermum jasminoides (star jasmine) varieties will give a relatively impressive show, requiring the backing of a wall or fence, where they will grip by themselves after a bit of initial support. Star jasmine is not very hardy inland in the UK – the best ones will be

found within 30km (20 miles) or so of the sea – unless it is given a particularly warm, sheltered position. It flowers best in a sunny location and enjoys a poor, gritty, well-drained soil. The toughest species is *Vinca* (periwinkle), a potentially invasive ground-cover plant in the UK. The family is Aponocynaceae.

Vitis (Vine)
L, SU, D, ACAL, DE.

Vines are predominantly used as internal boundaries between different areas of the garden, trained along posts and wires. Generally, they are quite large-leaved in the growing season, while in the winter the structure will feel very bare. There are many varieties available. Not all of them are equally hardy and the final choice will be down to personal preference. Fabulous in stony sandy soils, they need good drainage. The vine is related to plants such as *Parthenocissus* or Virginia creeper, in the Vitaceae family. Plenty of good ventilation and spacing to allow air movement will help reduce mildews on new growth.

Vitis.

Wisteria.

Wisteria
L, SU, D, ACAL, DE

Wisteria is best suited to pergola systems, rather than boundaries, unless it can be trained along long sections of trellis. It should not be planted into other living supports and it can restrict and smother host plants. Generally, they are pretty vigorous. They are related to the pea in the Leguminosae family.

CHAPTER 5

PLANTING AND TRAINING

Preparation for Planting

When planting a living divide, it is vital that the preparation is thorough and helpful to the type of plant being introduced to the ground. Preparation is always important in all types of gardening, but working with large plants, which is often how hedges and living boundaries are started off, has its own set of complications. Gardeners are taught to do the hard graft

themselves before planting, so that young plants do not have to. You need to understand that, however big the plants are when you buy them, they are babies again once they are taken out of their pots and put into the ground. This is because they are no longer established, so it is critical that their root systems are given every chance to grow well and strongly. If a plant has grown to a certain size in a garden environment, its root system will have spread over a much greater area in terms of depth and width than it would have in a pot. The plant that has been allowed to establish itself in a garden is much better equipped to find moisture and achieve stability more readily.

The golden rule when transferring a plant from a pot is to dig a hole twice as

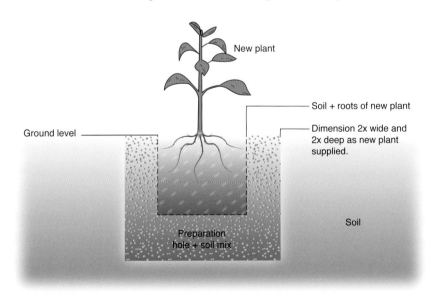

New plant

Soil + roots of new plant

Dimension 2x wide and 2x deep as new plant supplied.

Ground level

Soil

Preparation hole + soil mix

The golden rule: dig a hole twice as wide and twice as deep as the plant's pot.

wide and twice as deep as the pot in which it was supplied. In theory, then, if the pot is a foot wide and a foot deep, you will need a hole two feet wide and two feet deep. If the pot is only four inches wide but a foot and a half deep, the hole will need to be eight inches wide and three feet deep. If you buy a plant in a pot from a grower, you will see the way its root system naturally would like to travel, although it will have been restricted. Almost more than anything, it will appreciate being put into a soil that is loose and easy to penetrate. Where the hole is difficult to dig, and you cannot bring in extra equipment to break up and soften the ground to the appropriate dimensions, the results are bound to be slower. Nature insists that the roots of a plant must be established ahead of the tops. It stands to reason therefore that, if the roots are struggling below ground, the show above ground will be delayed. Plants that are artificially fed for healthy-looking growth above ground only are more likely to suffer in dry periods and will need lots of extra watering to help them.

When considering what size of plants you want to start with, remember that a large plant in a large pot will need a huge hole. Is there enough room to make holes of the right size all the way along the boundary? Thirty per cent of the soil from the hole should be kept to go back in with the plant, mixed in with composts and new soil from elsewhere. The bottom of the hole will need to be refilled loosely, so that the root systems can travel easily through the soil.

Bare-Root and Rootballed Plants

During the winter, it is possible to buy plants in a bare-root or rootballed state, to be transplanted into the garden. These plants have been grown in the fields and are lifted in the cold months for selling through nurseries and other suppliers. In bare-root form, they are dug up from the field without any soil – this is suitable only for deciduous, hardy plants. Evergreen plants that are field-grown need to be rootballed. In this case, they are supplied sometimes wrapped in netting, in a hessian or plastic bag containing soil around the roots at the base of the plant. Bare-rooted deciduous plants are watered regularly by the growers once they have been lifted from the fields and are usually provided in some sort of loose sacking to stop the roots drying out completely. The bigger the bare-rooted plant you buy, the more likely it is to have been lifted and re planted several times in its life already. This will have been necessary in order to maintain the capillary roots or young roots at the base of the plant, so that it can be transplanted successfully into a garden.

When planting bigger plants in bare-root form, you can orientate the root system carefully around an already positioned tree stake, in the half back-filled hole. This

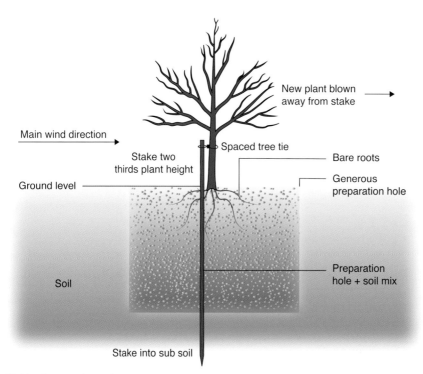

Main wind direction

New plant blown away from stake

Stake two thirds plant height

Spaced tree tie

Bare roots

Ground level

Generous preparation hole

Soil

Preparation hole + soil mix

Stake into sub soil

Staking bare-root specimens.

Rootball planting.

New plant

Remove wire + loosen ties
on rootball once in position

Ground level

Dimension 2x wide and 2x
deep a root ball

Soil

Preparation
hole and soil mix

should cause minimal damage to the root system. Smaller bare-root plants being arranged in a trench system for a hedged boundary will need plenty of loose soil to grow into, as they have nothing to draw from to get them going. Generally, growers will lift deep-rooted, bare-root plants later in the winter months, as moisture will have penetrated further into the ground by then. Shallower-rooted plants will be lifted from the fields first.

Evergreen conifers and shrubs will often be supplied as rootballed plants, with some of the field soil still on them. This provides them with a reserve of nutrients and moisture around the roots – evergreens will die if they are allowed to dry out at all. Sometimes, suppliers will buy bare-root and rootballed plants and then containerize them. This speeds up the container process, as field-grown stock is quicker than pot-grown. It also allows the nurseryman to compensate for any losses in field-grown stock, which are more likely to fail than container-grown plants, due to the root disturbance. For example, when planting box (*Buxus*) in a boundary, it is advisable to use either container-grown or one-year containerized plants. A one-year containerized plant has been lifted in the field and transferred to a pot a little bigger than its roots, with some fresh compost, and grown on for a year from the time of being lifted. This form is more suitable when including box in a boundary or hedge, because box is very slow-growing, evergreen and

small. It is often offered as bare-rooted plants, but evergreens should not be purchased in this form. It is suitable only for hardy, deciduous plants.

Rootballed plants should be lowered into the hole that you have prepared and the netting or hessian loosened around the neck of the rootball and cut away where possible. Do not lift up the plants, as they would then be unsupported rootballs. Take great care not to snap any roots that are still attached to the new plants.

Digging and Staking

On very heavy soils, you will need to dig your holes with a border fork, which will tear its way through the ground and not 'smear' the inside of the hole, as the blade of a spade would. This will enable good root transference from hole to surrounding soil, as the new plants grow and establish.

Larger plants often need a stake to support them. If this is the case, it is best to put the stake in position while the hole is open and before the plant is put into the hole. The stake should always be on the same side of the hole as the source of the prevailing winds, so that, when the strong winds blow, they will hit the stake first and lift the plant away from the stake. If the stake is on the wrong side, it is likely to allow parts of the plant to rub on the stake and as a result there will be a greater potential for disease. If the stake is put in

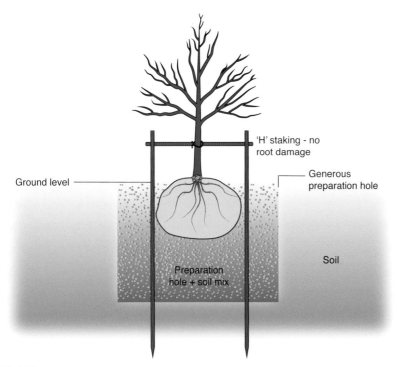

'H' staking - no
root damage

Ground level

Generous
preparation hole

Soil

Preparation
hole + soil mix

H-staking.

Staking using two stakes and middle tree ties.

while the hole is open, it can go into the subsoil which is undisturbed and will grip the stake much more success-fully. Another reason for put-ting the stake in before the plant is to avoid driving it through any new roots on the plant, or causing any other damage to it while trying to knock the stake into place.

Really big root systems often require an 'H' stake sys-tem, which is basically two stakes and a crossbar. The plant is tied in to it using tree ties affixed from the crossbar. This allows you to put the upright stakes in either side of the big roots and not damage any of them in the process. Again, the crossbar should be on the side of the plant that the prevailing wind will hit first, so that the plant is blown away from it, thus reducing the risk of rubbing and disease. After staking at roughly half to two-thirds of the height of the plant, for the first year and then the next few late winters, it is good to reduce the stake by a third and re-affix the tie. This means that the plant is still being held securely, but that there is an increased 'sail effect' on its branches. This, in turn, sends a strong message to the root systems to work harder to support the plant. From that time on, for the next couple of years, the stake height should be reduced annually at around the same time – the end of winter – to encourage the root systems to continue to strengthen themselves against the increased sail effect. Too often, gardeners leave stakes at their original height and then remove them completely after four years or so. Within a short time, after just a few stormy days, the plants will start to fall over. This is directly due to the taller stakes having over-supported the new plants, and preventing the root systems getting the message that they needed to develop to the point at which they could support the plant without any artificial help. A taller stake will reduce the amount of buffeting that the plants receive, and this will send the wrong message from above the ground to the system below the ground – the stake is doing the work that the plant needs to learn to do itself.

Sometimes, on a bigger project, it will be necessary to bring in a digger and create a large trench for planting, in order to get the spacing correct for the particular cultivars that are being introduced to the boundary. Nowadays, professional landscapers have access to powerful, very narrow diggers, which can usually squeeze into back gardens, even where space is limited. Hiring a contractor to do the more substantial, difficult jobs may seem a bit expensive, but it is almost always better than tackling it yourself, unless you have extensive experience. If you can find someone who really knows their stuff and has the right equipment, they will be able to do a much tidier job than you could, in a much shorter time. As well as saving money in the long run – you are less likely to have to carry out remedial work later – you will enjoy the peace of mind that comes with knowing that the job has been done properly. If you are the professional, it is vital to make clear to a potential customer the importance of getting the preparation and planting part right, and to explain how this is reflected in any quotation that you give. Customers will sometimes go for the lowest quotation when selecting a contractor to work on their project, but will find out a few years down the road that their plants are struggling, because they have not recognized the need for proper preparation and the wisdom of paying for it. If it is a matter of just a few plants in a garden it is probably not too serious, but in a boundary situation it is imperative to get the right result first time round. When submitting a quotation, do not allow your customer to misunderstand or to be left to guess what you intend to do. This should reduce the risk of you not getting the work. There are no situations in which results are better with less preparation. Short-cuts almost always lead to a poor outcome.

Soils and Growing Mediums

When digging out holes for new plants, keep roughly thirty per cent of the soil back from them, so that it can be mixed with the correct composts to get the roots going well. The two main extremes of soils that gardeners have to deal with are very heavy soils (in other words, almost all clay) or very sandy and stony soils.

Heavy Soil, Clay

A heavy soil needs to be opened up to try to stop waterlogging in the winter and complete drying out and cracking in the summer. One of the most effective ways of dealing with this issue very quickly is to ensure you have plenty of gravel, grit, sand and other small particulates, as well as compost at the ready. When the garden experiences a dry summer and the ground cracks open, the particulates can be brushed into the cracks, to stop the ground sticking itself back together again the next time it rains. This will create aerated pockets for the roots of the plants to find. Clay does have all the nutrients, but they are generally locked up and not accessible to the roots, so these aerated pockets are very valuable to the plants. The particulates do not need to be at all nutritious for that reason.

The introduction of soil above the clay can also create a better-aerated medium for the plants to grow into (see Chapter 2 on mounds or bunds). The heavy soil then becomes the subsoil. It is still worth implementing the crack-filling trick before raising the ground, as the roots from the plants above can travel nicely into the gaps created by the backfilling in the summer.

Sandy, Stony Soil

Dealing with sandy, stony soils is a completely different ball game. If you left a hose running on the ground on sandy soil for a fortnight, the water would drain away, and there would still be no puddle. These conditions do not suit moisture-loving plants. Often, if a plant that needs lots of moisture finds itself in this environment, it will stretch its roots a lot further to try and find moisture, leading to a disproportionately wide-ranging root system. As sandy and stony soils do not hold any moisture, they are unlikely to hold any nutrients either, so they lend themselves to plants that enjoy poor soil, such as gorse (Ulex) and barberry (Berberis). If you do decide that you want to have something that is very hungry in its native condition, you will need to try to improve the soil considerably if it is to have any chance of thriving in the long term. One of the best ways is to introduce some heavy clay into the bottom of the hole that you have dug for planting. This will basically act like a perpetual sponge. As the roots grow down into the clay, they will hold on to much more moisture and, therefore, nutrients.

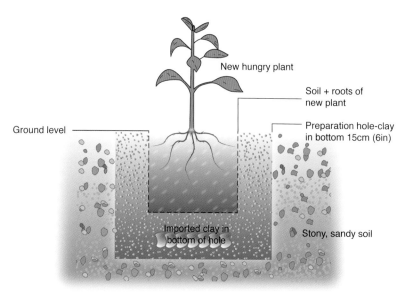

New hungry plant

Soil + roots of new plant

Ground level

Preparation hole-clay in bottom 15cm (6in)

Imported clay in bottom of hole

Stony, sandy soil

Planting hungry plants in stony soils.

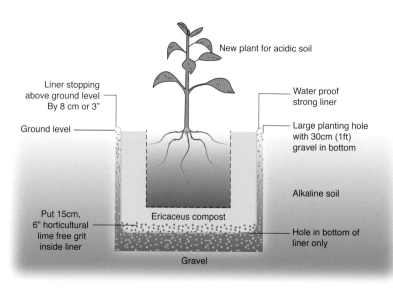

New plant for acidic soil

Liner stopping above ground level By 8 cm or 3"

Water proof strong liner

Ground level

Large planting hole with 30cm (1ft) gravel in bottom

Alkaline soil

Put 15cm, 6" horticultural lime free grit inside liner

Ericaceus compost

Hole in bottom of liner only

Gravel

Acidic bed in alkaline soils.

Another method of achieving nutritional hold in a poor soil is to add a really old mulch, from a tree surgeon's chipper – that is, basically woody soil – when it is approximately two years old. Mix it thoroughly in with the soil. If you have a garden soil that is somewhere in between, then adding compost mixed with the soil that it has to live in long term is a good way forward. The trouble with the method of adding old mulch is that the plants that really like poor soil are not used to the decomposition process that results from the decaying of old wood.

Acid-Loving Plants

Sometimes, specialist composts such as ericaceous are required for certain sets of plants. They are primarily used in containerizing plants – in the case of ericaceous, those that are acid-loving and cannot tolerate chalk. The danger is that the surrounding soil will not be compatible and therefore the plants will do well only for a short time, while they are growing in their own special compost. It is possible, though, to grow acid-loving plants in chalky surroundings, as long as you carry out the correct preparation. Basically, this means creating a hole or trench that is lined and filtered to ensure that lime from the surrounding ground cannot get to the roots of the acid-loving plants. The method is not cheap to implement, but it is very effective if it is done correctly, and will allow you to plant something that would not normally be seen in the vicinity. The materials need to be of a high quality – if you have a puncture within the cocooned root space that you are creating, lime will certainly leach into it, and the entire system will fall apart. Any failure such as this will be especially noticeable in a boundary, if one or two of the plants die out and the rest remain healthy because their membranes have not been compromised.

Building Debris

If the new plants are being encouraged to grow into an old building site full of rubble and building debris, it is important to mix some of the rubble into the hole with the new composts that the plants are going to grow through. If you were to dig a big hole and remove all the rubble from it, then fill it with the right compost for the plant, the roots will get to the side of the hole and will not be able to go any further beyond where you have dug. The roots will just go round and round within the hole, and this in turn can cause a lack of stability or ability to find moisture. After several years, the plant can literally just fall over. One more point to remember is that most building materials, such as sand, cement and rubble from bricks and blocks, contain lime, so growing lime-hating plants on old building sites can have its own set of challenges.

Fencing and Other Plant Supports

Posts and Stakes

Posts and stakes should be made from pressure-treated timber, as this will help them last longer than untreated ones. This is especially important for wood

Never use garden wire directly on plants.

Stake with tie.

Garden jute for tying in plants. It breaks down naturally and avoids plant damage.

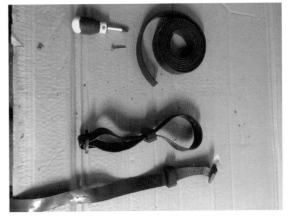
Tree ties.

that is going into the ground as it will rot very fast otherwise. There are three main types of stake: square, half-round and round. Different types are used in either directly supporting new plants individually, within the garden boundary, or as divide posts for a trellis, or wires or crossbars to which the plants are tied. Plants should be tied on to wire using jute, which is a natural product, while tree ties should be used to tie them in to wood. (A small tack or wood screw through the back of the tree tie into the stake – the inert wood that is supporting the plant – is a good way of stopping the tree tie from moving around in windy conditions.) Tree ties should be used when tying thick branches and trunks, and jute when tying in the smaller branches and twigs. Never tie too tightly. Plants always need to be able to move within the ties, thus allowing for expansion, especially in the most active growing months of the year. It is better to tighten tree ties just as the winter begins and loosen them again in early spring. The plants will not be trying to grow through the winter months and will benefit from a tighter grip to help protect them against the impact of heavy winds. With the arrival of spring, they will be trying to grow again and they will need that little extra room for expansion.

If you are staking trees directly with one stake per tree, running parallel to the trunk, it is advisable to use round stakes. In an ideal world, you always want to keep the stake from touching the plants at all, by using the spacers on the tree ties. If it proves impossible to prevent rubbing completely, less damage will be caused by round stakes against the trunks than any of the other types. If you are using the 'H' staking method to hold a tree within a boundary, it is good idea to use two half-round stakes for the uprights and the cross-bar. From an aesthetic point of view, the round and half-round stakes look much more natural up against the plants. The square and half-rounds, with their flat surfaces, are excellent for the purpose of fixing wires and crossbars. Square posts are available with chamfered bottoms to go into the ground, but they may have to be shaped further in order to drive them in properly.

Another method uses metal spiked fence post bases, which stop the posts rotting off too quickly. These are often brown or green because the square part that holds the post is left just above ground level, and remains visible, while the lower part – the spike – is

in the ground. Another alternative is a short concrete post known as a godfather, to which the square wooden post is bolted. Keeping wood off the ground as much as possible and using more solid material, such as concrete or metal, actually in the ground will make the posts last longer.

Trellis

Trellis has three main functions: first, to support plants that are growing against an inert support, such as a fence or wall; second, to support plants above a fence or wall; and third, as an individual support for climbing plants, creating a stand-alone living divide. In the first instance, it is good practice to screw spacers to the wall or fence, so that the trellis is held away from it by a few inches. This allows the plant to grow and expand behind the trellis as well as through it. The second function uses nature to heighten a divide above an inert support, such as a fence panel or wall. For the third option, it is probably more important to have a

Ideally, trellis should be held away from a wall using equal-sized wooden blocks.

A trellis fixed above a wall, with planting space.

Stand-alone trellis.

Metal mesh.

thicker, closer network of battens within the trellis, in order to maximize the support of the climbing plant. Remember, climbing plants without support are really ground-cover plants and their branches are therefore lax in habit and need regular tying in. Natural jute is ideal for this type of divide work.

Metal Mesh

Mesh is usually available in galvanized or coated metal and provides a fantastic divide for tying in climbers, especially if you choose climbing plants that will give flowers and fruit over a long period of time and will create spectacular combinations. The mesh also provides a more contemporary look and will certainly last for a long time. This type of mesh is often fixed to specialist metal posts in the ground, and is usually used to create stand-alone divides, rather than against fences or walls.

Canes and Hooks

If the wall behind wall shrubs or climbing plants is particularly appealing, and nice to look at in the short term, while the new plants are small, you may not want to hide it behind a large piece of trellis. One option is to use a system of brass hooks put into the wall via small holes with rawlplugs. Sturdy canes are then positioned horizontally into the hooks, one at a time, starting from the bottom. While the plants are very small, they are supported by just one cane and then, as they grow, the next cane up is inserted, and so

Cane and hooks system.

Training a plant using canes and jute.

Tying point on cane using jute.

on. This ensures that the wall is still a feature as the plants grow.

Climbing plants can be trained along the canes and in the long run a criss-cross of structure develops as each cane is introduced. This method often helps the climbing plants to flower more profusely, so that they fill up and soften the bottom half of the wall rather than migrating upwards too quickly. It can also easily lend itself to fan training.

Chicken Wire

Chicken wire is available in different heights on a roll. Its first use is to contain animals in a specific area. In this case, the chicken wire would be positioned behind the hedge being planted, so that it would have a natural green front as the hedge grows. The second use is as a barrier to wild creatures, such as rabbits and small deer, to stop them coming near the hedging plants while they are young and still establishing themselves. It should also prevent them coming into the garden and eating other plants – most wild animals are particularly keen on new growth.

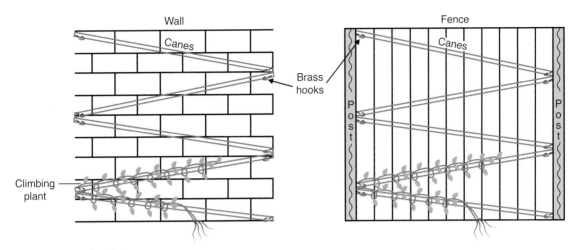

Canes and hooks for climbers.

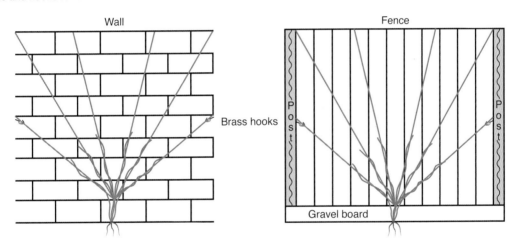

Canes and hooks for feathered wall shrubs.

Where rabbits are a particular problem, because they can burrow so effectively, it is better to bend the chicken wire back on itself at ground level. If the new hedge is located in a rear garden that is already generally rabbit-proof, you probably only need chicken wire on one side, to shield the garden from invasion from someone else's land. However, if you are planting a living boundary in a front garden, in a more open area, you may need to have chicken wire on both sides. This protection will give the hedge the best chance of growing into a strong boundary.

Chicken wire can be planted up very effectively with annual climbers and light-framed plants such as Group Two or Three clematis. As time goes by, you could allow the edge of the hedge system to grow through the wire and clip it regularly, almost back to the wire. This will ensure that small twigs are in contact with the wire. Do not let the hedging plants grow far through the wire mesh; as they become thicker and more woody, they will be damaged by the wire.

Stock Fencing

Proper stock fencing does the same as a chicken wire fence, but is effective against bigger creatures, such as larger deer. These animals can jump very high so stock fencing is often positioned close up to the plants that require protection, to prevent them getting

Chicken wire.

Green stock fencing in a roll.

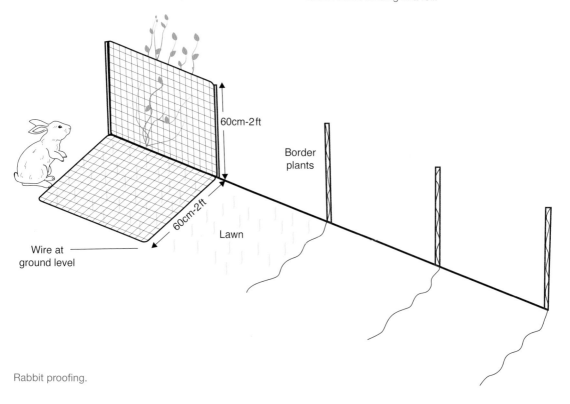

60cm-2ft

Border
plants

60cm-2ft

Lawn

Wire at
ground level

Rabbit proofing.

Stock fencing as a boundary for cattle.

Post and rail fence.

Post and wire fencing.

Chestnut paling fence.

Post and Wire, Post and Rail, Chestnut Paling

These three fencing options can be used for the middle part of a fedge (*see* Chapter 2). All three are nice and open, allowing plenty of space and air for healthy, unrestricted growth, and give a very natural look. Eventually they will disintegrate within the middle of the hedge, once it is established.

Sundries

- Brass hooks and vine eyes, for wire work. Screw into wood directly or drill and use rawlplugs for masonry.
- Various nails and staples, for wire work.
- Various wood screws for fixing wood to wood. A screwdriver is better for not dislodging posts than heavy sideways hammering.

too close. They may be able to reach a few leaves, but it will mean that they will be merely grazing the plant rather than destroying it. Again, stock fencing is available in various heights and it can be very effectively planted up with climbers. It also provides good tying-in points, using jute, for the young hedge on the other side.

Brass hooks.

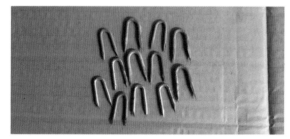

Staples for attaching wire to wooden posts.

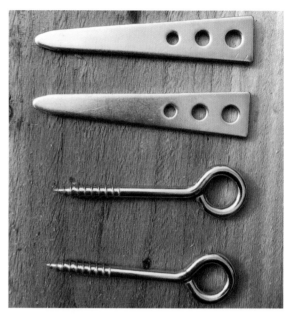

Seep hose for new planting schemes…can be hidden using mulches.

Vine eyes.

Tools

Hammers

It is sensible to wear a hard hat and safety goggles when using a hammer. The bigger the hammer, the more it hurts and the more damage it can do, should anything go wrong.

- Seep hoses are the best way of gently watering new and establishing hedge systems. Simply lay out along the planting just under the mulch layer.

Hammers.

Spades and shovels.

A claw hammer is really useful for the removal of unwanted nails and staples, as well as for straightening them and hammering them into place. A lump hammer is really a lightweight sledgehammer and more unwieldy than a claw hammer. However, it can be used in more restricted locations for hammering posts into place, while a full-size sledgehammer may be used in a more open site.

Post rammers are heavy and very good at driving round posts into the ground. Be careful not to lift it off the post while you are working with it, as it can easily slip off the top and come back at you.

Screwdrivers

Modern battery-driven screwdrivers are very efficient. The heads can be changed to suit the screws that you are using.

Spades and Shovels

Doing a job well and efficiently depends very much on having the correct equipment, and having the right

Fencing spade.

spade particularly makes a difference. The three most important spades for planting boundaries are the fencing spade, which is basically a very long-handled narrow-bladed tool for creating narrow, deep holes, the flat-ended border spade for moving and digging soil, and a pointed spade, usually with a short handle, so that it is easy to manipulate. You will need knee pads when using the latter, as it will be most effective when you are down at ground level. If you have lots of loose soil to shift, such as trench spoil, then a fourth type of spade will be a must: a shovel.

Forks

A border fork is really useful in a garden that has heavy soil. It can be used for loosening soil, ready to shovel out from the hole when creating a trench, or for digging a hole in clay-like soils. A 'ladies' fork', being narrow, is suitable for more intricate work and for loosening narrow holes. A wide fork is best for moving mulches.

Rakes

A soil rake is useful for finishing off an area and for applying mulches.

Forks.

Training

All the following training methods require regular work. If you are unable to give them the right amount of time, they will soon become a waste of money and the effect will quickly be lost. While plants are growing, the new growth is easy to tie into position, as it will be flexible. However, if the branches and shoots have already been growing in the wrong direction for a while, it will be much more difficult to get them to go where you want them to.

Fan Training

A fan-trained plant takes on a shape rather like a peacock's tail, where the middle of the plant at the base is the body of the peacock and the plant is its feathers. It is possible to buy plants that have already been started off in this shape by the grower, with a structure of canes. These are often young fruit trees or, in the ornamental world, wall shrubs such as *Ceanothus*, *Pyracantha* or *Cotoneaster*. Referring to one of these pre-started plants, you can get a grasp of what the grower has been doing, and you may be able start to do the same with any other wall shrubs.

Once you have decided on this type of arrangement, it is critical to choose the right plant for the job if you are to achieve a successful result. Whichever shape you want in the long run, you must have it in mind when you choose your young trainable plants. For fan training, you will need wall shrubs that are feathered with many breaks very low down. This means that you want plenty

Fan training.

of young branches, close to the base of the plant, so you can begin to arrange them out in a fan to start with.

The best supports for fan training are mesh and the fuller trellises, either stand-alone or against trellis spaced away from a wall or fence. These will provide lots of tying-in points for you and your ball of jute. Without a wall or fence, fan training would be more suitable for an internal divide, within a garden, rather than right on the boundary as a fixed living divide.

Espalier Training

Espalier training is very ornamental, but relatively easy to do if you are prepared to put the time in. The technique is more often used on fruit trees than on ornamental plants. Again, it is vital to choose the correct plant to start with from the many small tree and wall shrubs. It can be done very effectively with *Pyracantha* and *Cotoneaster*.

Espalier training can be done on a simple post and wire system or on canes on hooks against a wall or fence. It can be very striking against an attractive backdrop, because it will not obscure it in between the tiers. There may be three or even four tiers, usually with 30–45cm (12–18in) in between, as long as the plant has enough vigour. Only wall shrubs, with their deep roots, should be used next to walls, because of the footings. In an open situation, with no footings, small, ornamental trees with wider roots can be used to great effect.

When using small trees for espalier training, you need to find some that already have breaks or small branches low down on the plants. Ideally, the plant will have a trunk with side branches almost opposite each other, the bottom one about a foot off the ground, and the second about a foot above that. If there are branches in between these, they can easily be pruned back to the trunk. If they are not fully developed as branches, but there is at least some short growth, they can be trained quite nicely into tiers. Equally, if they are a bit too far developed for bending out horizontally from the trunk, they can be pruned back and, as the new growth appears from the pruning, this can then be trained into tiers.

Make sure you set up the tier supports at the planting stage, so that you have a framework to work to at the correct height for each tier. Avoid plants that have been top worked, where all the branches to five foot have been removed, as you will not be able to create the tiered situation that is required for espalier training. Visit the plant regularly and tie in the new growth as it appears. Regularly prune off unwanted growth to short spurs so that it flowers and fruits close to the lateral tiered branches, and is able to maintain its tiered habit. Keep the end growing points tied down regularly, on the horizontal supports that you have installed beforehand. The whole set-up will then develop into a strong, easy-to-maintain espalier.

Cordon Training

Cordon training is more often applied to fruit trees, but there is nothing stopping you using it on more ornamental plants. Generally, a cordon comprises straight

Espalier training.

Cordon training. The same system can also be used on a simple post and wire open fence without the backing of a wall. (Image by Andrew Martin from Pixabay).

plants trained at a 45-degree angle in a line, against wires between post supports. It can be a very effective divide in the middle of a garden, but is less good for an outer boundary as it is not full. The plants need to be pruned regularly, back to short spurs off the main trunks, and they will flower and fruit very close to the trunks as a result. As you are pruning back the laterals to short spurs, the top will grow out with more vigour and you will be able to keep tying that at a 45-degree angle. They may sometimes be as long as eight feet on a six-foot divide, because they are on the diagonal.

Step-Over Training

Step-overs are basically woody plants that have been divided into two low down, and then tied down on to ropes or wires only about a foot off the floor. The tied-down branches grow away from each other and nothing is allowed to grow upwards above them. The result is a low divide, which can be used to edge a path. The technique is quite widely used in the fruit world, but it can also be applied very effectively to other woody plants.

Layering

Primarily, layering is a way of thickening a mixed boundary that is already growing in situ. The plants are cut half way through their stems and then bent over and pegged down in a horizontal position. This is done in the winter. As the spring starts, the branches that have been laid down become trunks and start to produce new growth vertically. They still have enough energy in them to do this, because they were only cut halfway through. This technique is often used to fill gaps in a boundary, creating a good, thick stock-proof living divide. If you have never done layering before, it would be worth enrolling on a professional course, and then practising on a small section that does not matter very much.

Step-over training.

Close-up cut used in layering.

Layering.

CHAPTER 6

EXTENDING, MAINTAINING AND REHABILITATING EXISTING BOUNDARIES

It is sometimes possible to bring into line all the existing living boundaries in a garden, as long as you have an informed approach on how to go about it. Sadly, however, some existing living boundaries will have gone too far for any sort of rehabilitation to take place. This

Overgrown living boundary obstructing the pavement.

is often due to lack of maintenance over many years, or because a particular plant is untrainable or irretrievable after a certain point. This really highlights the importance of a correct programme of maintenance – failing to implement this will be more expensive in the long run, for several reasons. First, removing the old and growing the new takes time and much more money than the cost of many years of maintenance. Second, a new living divide will create new shade lines and the old ones will disappear once the old hedge or boundary has been removed. There may be plants in neighbouring gardens that will begin to struggle as a result of the change, and may even die. Third, the existing habitat will be temporarily lost, although a new one will be created, with time. The rehabilitation, or the removal and replacement of an existing divide should not be undertaken during nesting season. Fourth, planning permission from the local authority may well be required before any changes can be made.

Hedge ending. ideal for extending.

Extending an Existing Hedge

Extending a hedge that is already in position and well established sounds as though it should be easy, but there are a number of complications in tackling this job. There are at least nine questions you need to ask yourself before you do anything (assuming that the plan is to continue the hedge with the same variety of plant that is already there):

1. Is the hedge still going to do the job you require when it goes over a new piece of land? It may be deciduous now, but it may be more appropriate to have an evergreen boundary in the location of the extension.
2. Does it need to be extended towards buildings where previously it has been well away from them? This is massively important. For example, if the established hedge is made up of trees such as beech or *Fagus*, it will not be safe to plant a continuation of the same species up to any buildings, as the tree roots will be likely to cause damage over time. This is especially the case if the trees are left to their own devices, so that the sail effect increases and, consequently, there is a significant increase in the size of the root system too.
3. Is the extension of the hedge going to be travelling along a different elevation – in other words, going from on the flat, to up- or downhill? Some plants will have been happy with the level of moisture they have at present and this could change dramatically if the elevation changes to a sloping one.

4. Is the extension to the hedge moving from sunlight to shade or from shade to sun? This could be critical to its success. The plants in the established part of the hedge may love the position they are in now, but the same species might suffer from any change of light levels, one way or the other.
5. Are the plants in the existing hedge in a group that cannot be planted too close to the root system of another plant of the same family? If so, any extension using the same plants will not be successful, because the ones nearest to the existing hedge will fail to thrive. The new part of the divide will be only a partial success. One option is to leave a big gap between the existing plants and the next plant of the same variety, and to use different plants to fill the gap, but this will inevitably change the appearance of the hedge significantly.
6. Will the root systems of the end plants in the existing hedge be able to withstand the digging that will be necessary to put the next plant in the ground? Some plants really dislike root disturbance and you could end up damaging and losing the end plant when trying to plant a new one near it.
7. Is it going to be possible to achieve a consistent height across the existing hedge and the extension? Sometimes, the existing plants will deteriorate in the long run, creating different heights along the length of the whole.
8. Has the existing hedge been generally manageable? If you extend it with the same variety, will you be creating more work for yourself than you need to?
9. Do the moisture levels differ dramatically between the two locations of the existing hedge and the potential new one? Bear in mind that the established hedge may have dried out the ground around it, while there may be more moisture in the site further away from it.

This set of questions highlights the importance of looking carefully at some of the potential problems before embarking on a job that can turn into an expensive mistake. The need for a longer boundary can present you with an excellent opportunity to change direction, and perhaps to introduce a contrasting variety of hedge. *See* Chapter 3 for information on the wide range of hedging plants that are available, paying close attention to the growing conditions, and think carefully and clearly about how (and whether) to extend the hedge that you already have.

Extending an Existing Living Boundary

This is separate from extending an existing hedge, as there are often structures involved and different types of plants such as climbers and wall shrubs. Again, it is

A change in boundary materials can soften the end of a hedge or fence; planting where materials change can lessen the contrast.

wise to analyse what you have already have and consider carefully whether you actually want the main structural part to continue. For example, if you have a walled section, with plants growing against it, would you want that to continue or not? It would be quite costly if you wanted to extend the wall. If you have a situation where your extended boundary will come nearer to a narrow space or closer to a building, then it would be wise to consider a man-made support with climbing plants and wall shrubs growing through it or against it. The roots of these plants are much less likely to cause damage to foundations than those of trees.

It is important to consider right from the outset the long-term height of your new divide. If you decide to build a man-made structure and then grow plants over it, you may not need it to be as high as the one that is already there. It can be very effective, for example, to have an existing wall and then extend the divide with a fence and a super plant, strategically positioned between the change of material from wall to fence. In no time at all, it will look like it has always been there.

Filling in the Gaps in a Mature Hedge

There are a number of reasons why gaps might start to form within existing hedge systems. If you are presented with this problem, it is worth trying to find out exactly why the gaps are there before buying any more plants to fill them in. It is extremely annoying to find out that you have wasted time and money, because the remedy has not done what you wanted it to do. It is much better to get to the bottom of the problem beforehand. Gaps often begin to appear in established hedges over time. Sometimes, ivy is allowed to take over a few of the plants, which then start to get weak and die out. Sometimes, one or more of the existing hedge plants simply die for no apparent reason and a gap appears. Sometimes, this will be due to maintenance not being done at the correct time or in the correct manner. Sometimes, the hedging plants have been planted too close together and some start to die out as they lose the fight for the same piece of nutrient and light. Again, this can cause random gaps within a divide.

Whatever the reason for the appearance of the gap, you are then presented with the challenge of planting something into it that will fill it up, and do the job of its

Ivy thriving through a holly hedge.

Gaps in hedges.

healthy neighbours for the long haul. Sometimes, it may be better to let the branches of the two plants on either side of the gap grow towards each other, to fill the gap. You could help them along by tying them together loosely with jute string, temporarily until they fill the space. This method is often very successful and better than introducing a new plant to fight with the existing ones in an already over-crowded root space.

Do not make the mistake of attempting repeatedly to fill gaps with plants of the same variety. Too often, garden-centre horticulturalists see people return year after year for the same plants, ignoring the advice that has been given to them. One garden owner had a big existing hawthorn or *Crataegus* hedge, with three gaps in it. Every few years in the winter, she would buy bare-root 'quicks' – basically hawthorn whips or young plants. The advice every time was to get away from any plant related to the hawthorn – which is rosaceous,

meaning that it is related to the rose family – and use something completely different. She would take the 'quicks' home, diligently put a wheelbarrow full of good stuff around them, watch them grow reasonably well for two or three years and then see them deteriorate as the root system moved out of the imported compost. They could not compete with the very established hawthorns on either side of the gap. If she had used a plant unrelated to hawthorn – holly (*Ilex*), for example – it would have been very happy to grow into that space and fill the gap permanently.

Another issue is that, if the established hedge is a sun-loving one, and the gap you need to replant is very dark, due to the maturity and size of the hedge either side of the gap, it may be too shady for the matching plant to thrive in.

If there is a gap in a conifer hedge, many varieties will be brown where they have had no access to light. This can present its own set of problems for putting a conifer back into the same space. First of all, many conifers do not like being planted where their parents

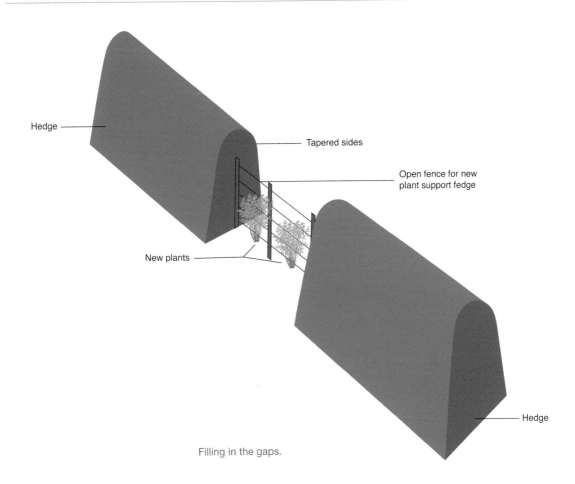

Hedge

Tapered sides

Open fence for new
plant support fedge

New plants

Hedge

Filling in the gaps.

have already been and, second, the light levels may not be sufficient to encourage the healthy growth into the gap of a plant of the same variety. In the case of a conifer such as yew (*Taxus*), however, the ends adjoining the gap will rejuvenate, and it will be possible to replant in the gap as the plant is fully shade-tolerant. Be aware, though, that the yew family is very slow-growing – the chances are that a mature boundary of yew will be many years old.

If the existing hedge is a mixed one, putting something different in to fill any gaps should mean that the new plants do not look out of place. This will allow you to select plants that will not be in conflict with the root systems of the existing boundary or interfere with its structure. Some hedging plants, such as *Escallonia*, support each other as they grow, so a new plant of this variety will need just a small piece of support within the gap for it to grow up and cover, almost like a mini fedge.

Maintenance of New Hedges

Maintenance varies, depending on whether the hedge is new or old. New ones may be trained, while old ones are probably set in their ways and will need more of a rehabilitation programme, often because of poor maintenance at some point in their earlier life.

When moving into a house where there is an existing new or young hedge, you will need to work with the legacy of somebody else's thought process and maintenance schedule. For example, they may have thought that they were going to grow the hedge to six feet, while you may hope it will reach seven feet. Neither is wrong, providing the plant that is there is capable of the dimensions that you are planning.

Any hedge or boundary needs to be right for the current owner of the garden, not the previous one. If it is young enough and you feel you want to make a radical change, or start again, it is important that you establish

Tapered hedge.

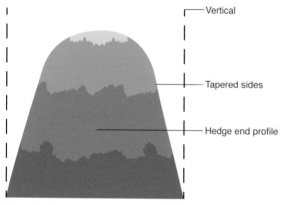

Tapering hedges.

the facts about the plants comprising it before you remove anything. Digging it out of the ground ready for new cultivars to go in can have serious implications.

Pruning is of course a vital part of any maintenance programme. Particularly with evergreens, the sides of the hedge should be tapered, so that it is narrower at the top and wider at the bottom. Moisture comes with prevailing wind and, if a hedge is vertical on its sides as well as being tall, the moisture will simply swirl about and land several feet away from the hedge. This will create an area at the base of the hedge that becomes increasingly dry, and will be almost impossible to plant up. Even the outside of the hedge down low can go brown, where the bottom of a vertical side is perpetually without natural moisture. A deciduous hedge may be kept vertical and tall, because it will lose its leaves during the winter months, allowing moisture to come

back to the base of the plants much more effectively than with evergreens.

With this type of taller hedge, it is a good idea to collect the fallen autumn leaves with a lawnmower on a high setting, then spread them out in a thin layer to break down naturally under the hedges. Leaves that have been chopped up by a mower will break down much faster than those that have been collected by a rake and then spread out under the hedge. If you have a conifer hedge, spread autumnal leaves from broad-leaf, deciduous trees beneath it, leaving them to break down. This will really help the hedge and allow you to under-plant or plant close up to the hedge more successfully. The more you neglect the base of a hedge, the fewer options you have for adding detail plants to nestle beneath it, and the more likely it will be that the base will become overrun with ivy.

Do not plant big structural plants directly in front of a conifer hedge. If it is the wrong cultivar of conifer, it will go brown and may not rejuvenate itself. Yew (*Taxus*) and western red cedar (*Thuja plicata*) can usually resprout where they have gone brown, but this can take a while.

Another factor with a young hedge is that the spacing on planting day does not always go according to plan. If for whatever reason you end up not being able to plant them all with the correct distance between them, you may need to train the plants to fill in any gaps, by tying them loosely with jute string. It is always better to do this than to have plants positioned too close together, so that they are for ever fighting below ground with each other for moisture and nutrients. This applies especially in a situation where a new hedge is in a narrow planting space, between two hard surfaces. Regular visits and pruning can be really helpful for training purposes. Because plants are live and ever-changing, they can be manipulated to a certain extent to achieve your desired goal.

Maintenance and Rehabilitation of Old Hedges

There are many scenarios relating to problems with old hedges, just as there are many cultivars of plant that are used for boundaries. Some literally cannot be rehabilitated and you will either have to live with the hedge – basically keeping it as it is – or remove it and

Living boundary beyond repair.. old and not maintained.

start again. If you decide to take it out and re-do it, this can have significant implications, particularly for the next set of plants to go in. Generally, if it is a big established hedge that has to be removed, the work will involve machinery and this will make it easier to do some significant preparation for the next planting. You

Laurel sprouting from very hard prune.

may have to remove a large amount of soil as you dig out the root systems of the old hedge, and bring in lots of fresh soil. This can be time-consuming and costly. However, preparation is everything and it is worth emphasizing that if this is not done properly, then the success of the next hedge system may be in jeopardy or at least not look good in the long term.

You should be aware that, in some areas, you may not be allowed to remove a hedge unless you have permission from the local council. In the UK, there are many situations where you need to approach the council for permission even to cut back a mature boundary, particularly where there are tree preservation orders (TPOs) in place.

In Chapter 3, the information about individual cultivars of plants used for hedging indicates whether they can be pruned hard or not. There are definitely some, such as cherry laurel (*Prunus laurocerasus*), that can be cut right back to ground level and will still sprout again from their base. Due to the mature root, they will grow into a new hedge that can then be pruned to the shape you require. The growth timeframe is much reduced, due to the mature root systems being left in the ground. It is worth allowing a section of cherry laurel to flower and fruit. The trouble with laurel is that its vigour makes people prune it often. (Incidentally, in the past gardeners were expected to use secateurs on cherry laurel, to avoid half-cut leaves.) It is definitely best suited to a medium-sized hedge – if it is pruned too often and kept too small, it will not produce its white buddleia-like flowers, which would usually be followed by its green, black and red berries. The fruits of the cherry laurel are nature's Christmas present for the birds, the first on the garden birds' winter wish list. They take the red berries and go, leaving the same truss to produce some more red ones a few weeks later, when the birds can revisit the same truss and take the next lot of red ones, and so on.

When pruning a *Leylandii* or × *Cupressus leylandii as a* hedge, it is vital to cut back only within the green or gold foliage, depending on the variety. If you cut back into brown foliage, the plant will never resprout again. The birds do value conifers to hide in when the weather is really cold, but they will not find many insects in there, so they do not linger for long.

With a mixed hedge, sometimes the layering trick (*see* Chapter 5) will help.

Another rule of thumb is to bring back or rehabilitate the older hedge over a period of years, rather than

A flail-cut *Berberis* hedge.

attempting to do it all in one hit. Generally, this means not taking off more than one-third of the plant at any one time, and then allowing it to recover and resprout lower down for at least a year. After that, you can do the same again the following year. Serious pruning such as this is usually done during the winter months in the UK. When dealing with evergreens, it is better done in the late part of the winter.

One of the difficulties with this kind of work is that wildlife can lose some of its habitat for a while. If a boundary is teaming with creatures, it is kinder to do any drastic cutting back towards the end of winter, making sure it is well before nesting time. Battering a mature hedge with flail machinery in the autumn will expose it to much more winter than leaving it alone until the end of January in the UK. When a hedge is left untouched for the winter months, it will harbour a huge amount of wildlife, providing protection, insulation and food for the overwintering insects and small creatures. This also brings them much nearer to the garden, field or orchard for pollinating, especially for the early flowers on edibles such as pear trees.

A climbing plant growing through a mixed hedge can be looking fairly unruly by the autumn. If it is in a location that is prone to snowfall, it would be wise to tie it back into the hedge frame for the winter using

Climbing rose in hedge.

Pyracantha in berry.

jute, especially if, for example, it is a rose that produces great hips for the birds. Snow can damage wayward branches that are too separate from the main framework, sometimes snapping them with the extra weight.

Another big problem with autumn pruning is that all the fruit disappears. This is food that could have been

Mahonia japonica.

fattening the birds up for the winter. It is worth observing that birds go primarily for the vibrant red fruits that appear early on in the season. This is why gardeners are advised to net their cherry trees and protect their strawberries – the birds just love what they produce. (Apparently, another way to keep the birds away – at least, more than 100 years ago – was to hang small hessian or muslin bags stuffed with human hair around the fruit trees.) Some varieties of firethorn (*Pyracantha*), for example, are grown for their red, orange or yellow berries. The birds will always strip the red ones first and then go elsewhere to get other red berries, before moving on to the orange ones a couple of weeks later, and then the yellow a few weeks later again. It stands to reason that introducing all sorts of reliable berrying shrubs, with a wide range of berry colours, amongst and under mature boundaries, especially hedges that are of one variety, the birds will be kept fed naturally throughout the winter. Some plants, such as *Viburnum tinus*, with its purply-blue berries, and *Symphoricarpus,* with its white berries, are still producing fruit quite late into the winter. Another reason why this is very successful is because many small garden birds tend to stay within sheltered plant structures and forage down low when the weather is cold. They are not often seen flying at sub-zero temperatures. Plants such as *Mahonia japonica* types should be left to flower and not dead-headed down low. The birds will definitely benefit from them in cold winters, as they fruit so well after their flowers have finished.

Mixed hedges come into their own in terms of the diversity of the wildlife they support, due to the range of varieties they contain. Each plant may attract certain insects, so it follows that having many different species of plants together in the same space, or in close proximity to each other, will mean having lots of different microorganisms and insects too. Many of these are beneficial to the garden, so providing them with the right habitat should be a consideration in all your gardening choices. With fewer and fewer natural habitats available for wildlife, every gardener can do their bit to encourage its presence, not threaten it further.

With changes in the climate, leading to milder weather in late autumn and early winter in the UK, hedges that have been recently pruned can produce new growth at the wrong time. This growth will be soft so that, when the weather does turn really cold, the hedge can suffer from die-back or, in the case of evergreens, the ends can go black for the winter.

CHAPTER 7

TREES AND CREATING STRATEGIC HEIGHT

The range of ornamental trees available for the garden is almost endless, so the list of varieties covered here is necessarily limited. It has been drawn up with boundary situations in mind rather than stand-alone situations. This is because many feature trees can be feature trees, adding a wow factor to a garden, only if they are given the space to show off their own particular characteristics. Special barks, silhouettes and habits can make excellent stand-alone features, but they can all be lost if the tree is planted into a living boundary, where it is then in a competitive environment.

Bare-Root, Field-Grown and Container-Grown Trees

The winter months are the time to acquire and plant bare-root and field-grown trees, while in the growing season they will be available from suppliers in containers. Where possible, the season from late autumn through to late winter is excellent for planting the varieties covered here. It is a time when the plants are able to put on a lot of growth below ground, expanding their root systems, while they are in a dormant state above ground. Most of the varieties can be bought as small, one- or two-year 'whips'; they do not need to be all the same height as the vigour will vary depending

on the variety. It is also possible to purchase larger trees and many sizes in between. The bigger the tree you buy in bare-root or field-grown form, the more important it is to know that the plant has been transplanted several times in its life time up to this point. It should then have produced plenty of capillary roots, close to its base. Be very wary of a tree in a bare-root state that appears to have sawn-off roots, and has very few fine roots or capillaries. It is probably not a good idea to buy that plant. The small roots are the ones that will take up the moisture and strengthen the tree once it has been planted in the garden.

Preparation needs to be very thorough and extensive when taking on bigger plants, whether it means more digging below ground or installing suitable support systems above ground. When you plant small, however, the preparation efforts and, therefore, the overall costs are reduced. Most small plants do not need stakes at the beginning (see the section on fedges in Chapter 2). Another huge advantage of starting a mixed hedge with whips is that you can allow one or two of the trees within the mix to grow tall, to rise above the hedge in the long run.

It is important to have a vision in your mind as to how high you want to keep a mixed hedge. Many of the plants will be trees, albeit some smaller than others, so they will have the capacity to make a taller living divide, in a strategic place anywhere along the length of the hedge. The joy of planting trees as whips within the hedge is that they allow you to create height, in time. This means that, should the need arise at a later date for strategically placed height, you will not have to buy a tree and dig intrusively into the hedge to plant it.

Suitable Varieties

Acer Campestre (Field Maple)

Generally, in the UK field maples are found in the mixed hedging section of the nursery, along with many other varieties. During the winter months they are sold in bare-root form. They are also available as one- or two-year-old plants, or whips, measured in centimetres. For example, you may see a label reading *'Acer campestre 60/90'* at the nursery, denoting a field maple that is 60–90cm (2–3ft) tall. They are totally chalk- or alkaline-tolerant and widely planted in the UK, although it is unusual to see them planted in a row or on their own. Field maples are not related to many other plants, but there are many hundreds of maples in the Aceraceae family. Some acers, being related to sycamore, can develop tar spot. The advice is generally to remove the fallen leaves in the autumn to reduce the risk of it returning the following year.

Acer (Maple)

The world of acers is huge, offering a wide range of separate trees to put into a hedge to create strategic height in the long term. The Japanese maple varieties are not ideal for the purpose of growing into living divides, unless you are in a sheltered, acidic woodland setting. Even then, it is wise to be careful when making your selection. One factor to consider when choosing a maple variety is the colour of the foliage, especially if you want to grow it above a hedge. Considering it in contrast to its surroundings could help you to maximize the effect in the long run.

Amelanchier (Snowy Mespilus)

Amelanchier canadensis is a very hardy, bushy shrub or small tree, which provides spectacular autumn colour and then loses its leaves. It requires neutral to acidic

Acer campestre.

Amelanchier in berry.

soil, and must be kept away from chalky ground. It has very showy new growth in the spring and masses of white flowers and reddish fruits soon after. It is capable of 12 to 15 feet in height. For a taller result, *Amelanchier lamarckii* is more upright in habit and capable of 20 feet in height. Both are often found growing above a shrubbery or hedgerow. *Amelanchier* is related to *Spiraea*, in the Rosaceae family, so it must be planted well away from any other members of the rose family, and not in a position where there has been a rosaceous plant before.

Betula (Birch)

Birch trees are wonderful, but it is vital to think very carefully at the outset about where they are to be positioned. If you have acidic or alkaline soil that is heavy and holds moisture well, birch can be a good choice, as they are thirsty and the root system will stay proportionate to the tree in terms of size. At the other extreme, if your soil is very free-draining, a birch tree within a hedge situation would cause the other plants alongside

Betula.

it to struggle unduly, as it would take most of the available moisture. It would also develop a disproportionately large root system, as the roots would travel further, to find moisture. The other point to consider is that a birch tree does not look very attractive when it has grown too large for the space and needs to be heavily pruned. It is important, therefore, to choose a variety that will go roughly to the size that you require in the long run. There are many varieties that only really work as stand-alone features within a garden.

Generally, young birch trees can take five to seven years before they really colour up on their trunks, as the small wood can appear quite grey. Many of them eventually have striking white trunks, but there are also bronzy-coloured ones and some with peeling bark. They also produce pendulous spring flowers then catkins of various sizes during the autumn and winter. If they do have to be pruned, it is best to do this in the dormancy of the winter months. They will often drip for days when pruned at the start of the growing season and when in leaf.

Many birch trees are field-grown and therefore available as bare-root or rootballed trees for sale in the winter months. For mixed hedging situations, it is possible to buy *Betula pendula* as whips during the winter. They are available from growers in the UK in various heights for hedge planting: for example, one grower may sell whips of 40 to 60cm, while another may sell 60- to 80-cm ones.

Birch is generally trouble-free, when planted in heavier soils. It is related to *Corylus* (hazel), in the Betulaceae family. Giving it a moist soil to live in will reduce its risk of illness; this will be increased when it is stressed, as it will be in dry soils.

Carpinus (Hornbeam)

Carpinus betulus, and its derivatives, are deciduous and are found in many parts of the UK. There are other ornamental forms, but not in common circulation. Traditionally, gardeners were taught that, if you hold a leaf of hornbeam up to the sky, its silhouette is the same as the shape that the tree will have in the long run, if it is not pruned. Facts like this are really useful for getting your head around nature's intention for a plant – when it is not interfered with by gardeners and their secateurs and saws. Hornbeams thrive in all moist soils, producing pendulous flowers in the spring and

Carpinus betulus.

Cotoneaster exburiensis.

then papery catkins in late autumn and winter. They are available in containers in the growing months, but are often supplied as field-grown whips and trees in the dormant season. In bare-root form, they start from small whips as short as 60cm, for immediate hedge planting, through many other sizes, depending on the grower, right up to big trees, which are then measured according to the girth of the stem 1 metre from the ground.

Generally trouble-free in moist soils, they are related to *Alnus* or alder, among others, in the Betulaceae or birch family.

Cotoneaster

The *Cotoneaster* is exceedingly versatile, featuring often in different types of living divide. As far as the tree section goes, there are two that are suitable. *Cotoneaster exburiensis* has white spring flowers, creamy yellow autumn fruits that develop a pink hue in the cold, and semi-evergreen foliage. It will reach a height of 3.5m (12ft) or so. *C. cornubia* has white spring flowers and red autumn fruits. It is slightly more

Cotoneaster cornubia.

evergreen and more vigorous (by about 1.5m, or 5ft), than *C. exburiensis*. These are the two most popular cotoneasters in the UK. They are best purchased as container-grown plants, as they retain some leaves in the winter months. This also means that you can hand-select the right ones for the job you have in mind. Be careful to plant them in soil that does not become waterlogged in the winter and away from any other existing rosaceous plants. Cotoneaster is related to *Pyracantha*, among many others, in the Rosaceae family.

Fagus (Beech)

There are many different types of beech tree for use within the garden. Some grow as natural columns, including *Fagus sylvatica* 'Dawyck', *F. sylvatica* 'Dawyck Purpurea' and *F. sylvatica* 'Dawyck Aurea', which are green, burgundy and gold, respectively. They can be positioned in the middle of a hedge when it is first planted, and then allowed to grow up to a height so that they punctuate the top in the long run. There are

Fagus sylvatica pruned to shape.

Fagus sylvatica left to grow freely.

Fagus sylvatica 'Dawyck Gold'.

also small, medium or large weeping beech trees with cascading branches, which are really best in stand-alone situations, showing off their unique form. *Fagus sylvatica* and *F. sylvatica* 'Purpurea' are the main two that are suitable for living divides. These are field-grown and therefore available in bare-root as whips

Fagus sylvatica 'Purpurea' pruned to shape.

Fagus sylvatica 'Purpurea' left to grow freely.

and trees, ready for planting as a hedge, or for growing up above a hedge. Both varieties become big trees over time, if left to their own devices. Related to oak trees, in the Fagaceae family, they are very happy on acidic and alkaline soils that do not become waterlogged.

When young, beech trees can show signs of aphids and mildews. When they are small, it is easy to deal with, but spraying a big hedge is not very environmentally friendly – the higher you have to spray, the greater the likelihood of spray drift, which can cause damage to other plants and even waterways. Beech also sometimes suffers from frost damage on its new growth, usually on the east-facing side. The more established the hedge, the more resistant it will be to these problems.

Laurus Nobilis (Bay Tree or Sweet Bay)

Bay is a valuable evergreen – obviously useful in cooking as well as in the creation of a solid living divide, particularly for those who live near the coast in the UK. Further inland in the UK, particularly in the Midlands and the northern regions, growing it outdoors without protection is much more difficult. When it is growing in an environment where it does not need protection, its basic requirements are very good drainage for its roots and a sunny position away from north and east winds. It is best to prune in mid- to late February. It seems to suffer more from problems with scale insect attack when it is grown in a pot or container than when it

Laurus nobilis does best in the south of the UK or near the sea.

grows freely in the ground. It should always be bought container-grown or rootballed if it has been field-grown. It has plenty of thick, upright growth and may even reach a height of 6m (20ft) in the southern parts of the UK, in and around coastal towns. It is related to *Persea americana* (avocado), among others, in the Lauraceae family.

Malus Sylvestris (Crab Apple)

A crab apple is a fabulous tree to incorporate into an edible living divide, with fruit that is frequently used in hedgerow recipes. It is related to strawberries, amongst many others, in the Rosaceae family, so it needs to be planted into good clean ground which has no remnants of any plants from that family. It needs a well-drained soil in a sunny location when it is first planted. It is typically available in bare-root form in the winter in the UK, in various whip sizes (40 to 60cm, or 60 to 80cm, for example), depending on the grower.

Quercus (Oak)

There are many varieties of oak available, growing into different shapes and thriving in various soil types. In terms of living divides, the deciduous *Quercus robur* (the English oak) and the evergreen *Q. ilex* (holm oak) are probably the most relevant.

The English oak is often sold in the form of field-grown, bare-root whips in the winter, usually in the mixed hedging section at the nursery. It may also be purchased as a bare-root tree. It is rarely planted as a hedge on its own; usually, it is planted in among other species within the hedge. English oak is long-lived and fabulous for wildlife. Although it is slow-growing, it is amenable to gradual training so that it rises to a strategic height above the hedge. *Q. robur* 'Fastigiata' is an upright, columnular form, which is great for punctuating a hedge system, in the long run, when planted at the same time as the rest of the hedge. It is happy on both alkaline and acidic soils, but it does need good drainage. It is related to the beech tree, in the Fagaceae family.

Malus sylvestris.

Quercus robur.

Q. ilex (holm oak) is an exceptionally tough variety, once established. It is similar to *Q. robur,* but evergreen. Because of its root system, it is generally sold in containers, even as a small plant. It is salt-tolerant, and therefore thrives near the sea, where it can become very dense with age. It grows into a big tree, so it is important to take care when considering its planting position. There are some massive specimens in the Midlands in the UK, as well as nearer the seaside.

Prunus Domestica Institia (Bullace)

Bullace or damson trees are often found in wild hedgerows and are excellent to grow near the vegetable plot in the garden. Its fruit are useful for hedgerow recipes.

Sorbus (Mountain Ash or Rowan)

Sorbus aucuparia, the common mountain ash, is frequently found growing happily all over the UK, in both acidic and alkaline soils, and in many really exposed areas. It is fantastic for wildlife, with a mass of flowers

Sorbus with yellow berries.

that attract the insects in the spring, and then the berries in the winter, which are much appreciated by the birds. There are many very attractive ornamental varieties, with a huge range of berry colours, from reds and oranges through to pinks and whites. Because they are members of the rose family, they must be planted well away from other rosaceous plants. *S. aucuparia* can be found as bare-rooted whips in the winter, which are suitable for planting into a mixed hedgerow. Many *Sorbus* varieties are trained at the growers, and not available until they are much bigger than whips.

Creating Strategic Height

When you mark out a living boundary prior to planting, at the planning stage, try to imagine the situation many years ahead. Is there anything that you need to hide or soften, from any particular viewpoint in your garden, or from any of the windows in the house? Never underestimate the results that can be achieved when these issues are considered and addressed at the outset. Careful planning and consideration of such scenarios is the best way to ensure that, a few years on, the garden will have become a real haven for the occupants.

Strategic height above a living divide can give a sense of framing a nice view, perhaps from an upstairs window, as well as obscuring something unsightly. Be sure to have a think about all the possible viewpoints well in advance of planting. Unless you have thought about it beforehand, once the hedge is all planted and nicely maturing, it will be too late to train one tree a bit

Prunus domestica insititia (bullace).

Pleached lime, creating strategic height.

higher than the rest, to enhance that view from the bedroom.

Strategic height can also give a very effective finish above mixed hedging, perhaps when the same plant is used at regular intervals and trained the same. For example, in a living boundary space of twenty-one metres, you might consider planting an *Elaeagnus* × *ebbingei* hedge, with an ornamental mountain ash every three metres. These could be container-grown, for planting at any time of the year, or field-grown, for winter planting. You might choose a mountain ash that

has fiery autumn colours, such as *Sorbus* 'Joseph Rock', to contrast with the *Elaeagnus* below.

Pleaching can be a way of getting height into a hedge, while keeping it narrow. One issue to consider is that most ready-done pleaches are carried out with deciduous trees and therefore provide only partial blocking in the winter. Being trees, they also have bigger root systems, so they may not be planted near the garden's infrastructure of walls and buildings. This might mean that you need to train it yourself, using plants such as *Cotoneaster cornubia*.

CHAPTER 8

COMMON PITFALLS

It is important to be thorough in your approach to and execution of your projects, especially when they are projects that are outside of your everyday experiences and working environment. One of the problems with horticulture is that it deals with such a vast array of plants from all over the world, so nobody has all the answers. In addition, there are so many variables involved in every gardening venture: moisture levels, soil types, pests and diseases, previous plants, new plants, chemicals, and so on. All will have a bearing on the results of any gardening project, and some are less controllable than others. However, there are a number of common issues that tend to come up time and again, and it will pay to be forewarned so that you can guard against them and, hopefully, find some effective remedies.

Wrong Plant, Wrong Place

Probably the biggest pitfall that boundaries fall into is the selection of the wrong variety of plant for the wrong location, together with a failure to implement the right programme of maintenance.

Example 1

The wrong plant is selected to grow next to a garden wall or building, time passes, and the stonework starts to crack as a direct result of the

Example 1 – the wrong plant positioned near a garden wall.

Example 1 – cracked garden wall.

development of the plant's roots. This can take quite a few years – often, the garden owner may not even recognize their mistake while they are still living at the property. *See* Chapter 3, for information on suitable plants for particular locations. Wall shrubs have deep roots.

Example 2

The wrong plant is put in too close to a hard surface, which starts to be lifted after time by the root systems. The classic here is the appearance of big cracks in driveways, paths, terraces and pavements. Again, the damage takes time to appear and is often a legacy of somebody else's planting.

Example 3

The planting is done without determining exactly where the amenities go, particularly sewage and water pipes. If the wrong plants are put in within the vicinity of drains and water pipes, and there is a leakage of any kind, the moisture-seeking root systems will gravitate towards the moisture source and then eventually find their way in, causing a lot of damage. It can be a costly mistake, so moisture-seeking plants should be avoided in such situations.

Example 2 – roots cracking and lifting hard surfaces.

Example 3 – moisture-seeking plants include willow.

Example 4 – *Buxus* (box) removed from a box hedge around an old vegetable garden plot.

Example 4

Buxus (box) makes an ideal low hedge along a path or around a parterre, where the ground tends to be undisturbed. It is less suitable for use around a vegetable plot, where regular digging is more likely to interfere with the roots. Root disturbance can make box more prone to blight, which is a particular problem with this species. Box should also be planted where its roots will have good drainage.

Example 5

If you are trying to make a boundary do a particular thing, you need to use the right cultivar of plant for the job you have in mind. The most common mistake is planting trees as opposed to shrubs, even though you only want a hedge to be shoulder height, or even less. It is vital to look at the likely long-term outcome before making an informed choice.

Example 6

Planting the wrong hedge in soil that has previously hosted a living divide. The pre-existence of plants of a certain family will directly affect your plant choices,

Example 5 – beech being kept to 120cm (4ft).

especially when none of the soil has been changed. It is important to be thorough in your assessment and preparation.

Example 7

Planting a wrong plant divide for the soil type, and getting a weak, just-about-living hedge. *See* the listings in Chapter 3 to find the right plants for particular soils.

Maintenance and Use

Example 8

Where the wrong plant has been positioned in a space that is limited – next to a pathway or a narrow entrance – it can begin to encroach on that space as it develops. As the plant forms the boundary, it is very difficult to keep it looking good and still filling the space in an attractive way. It might be deemed necessary to remove all the lower branches with foliage on,

Example 8 – most boundary trees will not resprout when their lower branches have been removed.

to just above head height, on a plant that cannot rejuvenate. The result will be trunks and branches with no foliage on, just at the point where the eyes are focused on. This will be unattractive, as well as leading to a loss of privacy. *See* the listings in Chapter 3 to find shrubs that can be kept narrow and full from low down.

Example 9

If maintenance has been sporadic over a number of years, especially on a planted boundary of the type that needs lots of attention, the result will be a sprawling, hacked-at mess. This is definitely not neighbourly. If you know that your time for maintenance will be limited, you should choose only plants that can recover from any inconsistency in care.

Example 10

Sometimes, garden owners use boundary trees as fence posts, nailing wire into the trunks and putting proper fence posts in between. If the nails or staples are never removed from the trees, they will keep growing and make a callous around the wire. Eventually, this will cause serious damage to the tree, as the wire will block the transport of water and nutrients to the plant.

Example 11

Trellising needs to be fixed out slightly away from its inert support. If there is insufficient space between the trellis and the wall or fence supporting it, with time the woody structures of a climbing plant will twine around and try to grow behind the trellis, forcing their way between it and the inert support. If this is not spotted soon enough, big sections of the plant can suddenly die off, as its water and nutrient transport system is blocked by the trellis. Put blocks on the trellis corners from the outset to bring it out from the wall.

Example 12

When trellis is being used to support wall shrubs, such as *Rhamnus alaternus* 'Argenteovariegata', or Italian buckthorn, it is better to tie the branches to the

Example 9 – an unmaintained boundary.

Example 11 – insufficient trellis spacing.

Example 10 – tree grown around wire.

trellis, rather than tucking them underneath. Often, the wall shrub will develop chunky branches, which can become quite sickly after a while if they have a battle with the trellis. They need to be tied on the outside using jute string – always have some of this in the shed, as you will find you will need to use it regularly.

Example 13

Do not be over-enthusiastic in using a leaf blower or rake to get rid of every bit of detritus at the bottom of an old hedge. Instead, leave it to break down. You could even add another layer of old composted leaves to the base of the hedge each autumn.

Pruning

Example 14

Many living divides begin as variegated, but, because a large number of variegated plants are sports of their green parents, they are susceptible to what is called reversion. If this is not kept in check, the green colour can take over. The green plants are generally more vigorous than the variegated versions, and sometimes vary in their habit. Make regular checks and remove plain foliage when it should be variegated. Remember,

though, that some plants, such as *Elaeagnus*, take time to develop their variegations.

Example 15

Pruning hedgerows at the wrong time of year is a common mistake. It is important not to do this, as it will reduce the extent of habitat that is available for wild creatures to use in the winter months, when they so desperately need every bit of help they can get. This is especially the case where so much of the natural habitat has been overtaken by man-made infrastructure. Another relevant issue is the existence in urban areas of 'green waste' bins, so that large quantities of garden debris are carried away by councils, rather than being left to break down in a corner of the garden. Wildlife needs a quiet, still place to thrive. Wood needs to be broken down over many years, so that it is almost mushy, before creatures such as the stag beetle can make use of it and live off it. There is a reason why the head count and range of insects is greatly increased in

Example 14 – reversion on *Elaeagnus*.

Example 15 – hawthorn left unpruned for the winter. It is fabulous for wildlife.

older mixed hedgerows rather than in the very young ones. Remember to prune in late winter not autumn.

Example 16

Over-pruning conifers that do not rejuvenate will encourage them to be brown. Regular light trimming is fine, but over-zealous cutting back just once a year will cause problems. Vigorous conifers such as *Leylandii* can put on up to as much as three feet in a year. They need light to keep them green, but this can penetrate only a foot or so into

Example 16 – pruning conifers too hard results in often irreparable damage.

the tree, so taking the top off in an annual chop will result in an ever-widening hedge. This is wrong for the plant. Regular, lighter pruning – say, three times a year – will enable you to keep on top of it and maintain it as a narrower plant or living divide. Of course, there may be cost implications in this, so perhaps you might decide – preferably at the planning stage – that a vigorous conifer is not the right plant for the job. There is no such thing as a fast-growing small plant. If it grows fast, it wants to be big. If it grows slowly, it is likely to stay small; if it does get big, this will only happen after many decades. The slower the plant, the easier it is in terms of pruning.

All Situations

Example 17

Do not fall into the trap of buying a living boundary solely on the basis of cost, rather than being careful to select the right plant for the job. Certain plants may seem to be less expensive at the outset, but when it comes to a living divide, the initial outlay should be balanced out with the fact that it may well outlive you. Generally, the cheaper the plant, the less time the nursery has devoted to it. A pocket-money price for a three-foot plant implies that it is a fast grower. It is better to buy small examples of the right plant, and spend much more money on thorough preparation and planting ingredients than on the plants themselves. If you follow that approach, the plants are more likely to thrive. Buying much bigger plants and trying to save money and effort on good preparation and careful planting is a false economy, as the plants may struggle for many years before they really get established. Remember: preparation and the correct start will make all the difference.

Example 18

Be wary of bamboo. It may start off as clump-forming and then get way too tall for the job. If you

Example 18 – bamboo encroaching on next door's territory.

then try to cut it back severely, it will start growing epicormically – that is to say, it will grow away from the middle at root level, and take up an ever-increasing amount of ground. The powerful roots will sometimes cause damage to walls, fences, patios and drains, and may even migrate next door, upsetting neighbours. Be very careful when planting bamboo on a boundary, to ensure that others are not adversely affected, and think about the unseen menace that it may become ten or fifteen years down the line. *See* Chapter 3 for specific information on bamboo.

Example 19

When you move into a new house, you may not have the same requirements from a living boundary as your predecessors. You may want to make some significant changes, to get the boundary to suit you going forward, but you should look at all options carefully before taking drastic action.

Example 20

Hasty decisions and actions lead to poor results. Thoroughness pays out in the long run. Do not rush the process.

INDEX